# PRAYER AS A WEAPON

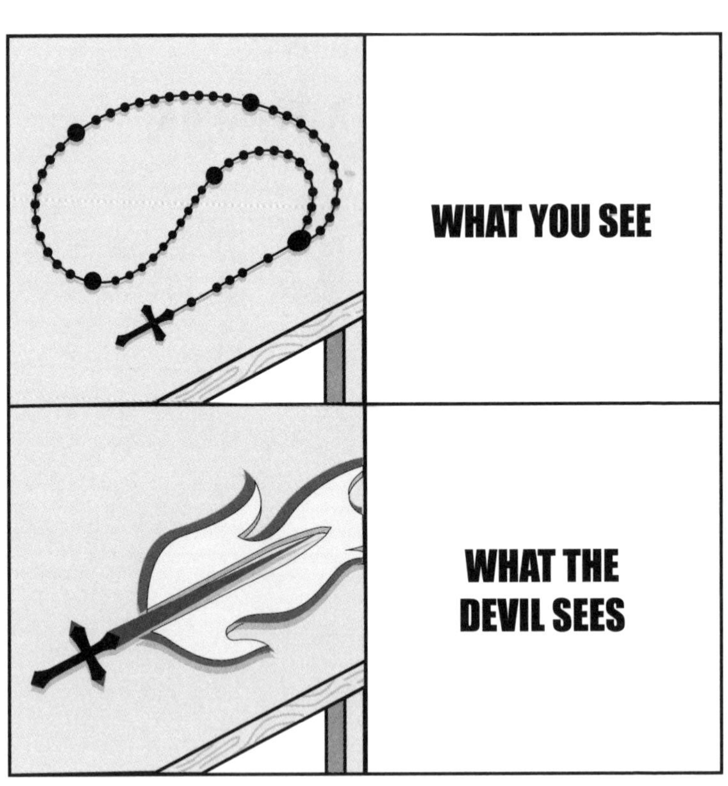

WHAT YOU SEE
WHAT THE
DEVIL SEES

Jesse Romero

# PRAYER AS A WEAPON

## HOW TO PRAY LIKE A JOYFUL WARRIOR

SOPHIA INSTITUTE PRESS

Manchester, New Hampshire

Sophia Institute Press
Box 5284, Manchester, NH 03108
1-800-888-9344
www.SophiaInstitute.com

Sophia Institute Press is a registered trademark of Sophia Institute.

Hardcover ISBN 979-8-88911-314-0

ebook ISBN 979-8-88911-315-7

Library of Congress Control Number: 2024946251

*First printing*

*"Blessed be the Lord, my rock, who trains my
hands for war, and my fingers for battle."*

— Psalm 144:1


*"Judas and his men met the enemy in battle with
invocation to God and prayers. So, fighting with their
hands and praying to God in their hearts, they laid
low no less than thirty-five thousand men, and were
greatly gladdened by God's manifestation. When the
action was over and they were returning with joy, they
recognized Nica'nor, lying dead, in full armor."*

— 2 Maccabees 15:26–28

# Contents

# PART III
## Annotated Quotations

# Prayer as a Weapon

# Introduction

## A Warning and a Mission

On September 11, 2001, God gave us a great warning. He allowed the double symbols of American money and military power to be attacked. Yet despite the faith that modern society places in these two ideas, no amount of either of them can ever restore America back to its original twin pillars: religion and morality. With 9/11, God put the question to us clearly: Will we continue to head toward the precipice of destruction, putting our faith in things that cannot save us, or will we turn back to God?

The blind leading the blind is an apt description of the current government leading the United States, especially when it comes to such issues as subsidizing abortion and legislating homosexual "marriage." Our situation may seem grim, but don't despair. The word on the street is, there's a Galilean named Jesus. He *is* the Word, and He can make the blind see. When we look at Him, and then we turn and look at what the government leadership and society around us embrace, we can see that the battle line has been drawn clearly: We can choose Christ, or we can choose chaos. Put differently, we can choose life, or we can choose death and destruction. Moses issued this challenge long ago, in Deuteronomy 30:15–20:

See, I have set before you this day life and good, death and evil. If you obey the commandments of the Lord your God which I command you this day, by loving the Lord your God, by walking in his ways, and by keeping his commandments and his statutes and his ordinances, then you shall live and multiply, and the Lord your God will bless you in the land which you are entering to take possession of it. But if your heart turns away, and you will not hear, but are drawn away to worship other gods and serve them, I declare to you this day, that you shall perish; you shall not live long in the land which you are going over the Jordan to enter and possess. I call Heaven and earth to witness against you this day, that I have set before you life and death, blessing and curse; therefore choose life, that you and your descendants may live, loving the Lord your God, obeying his voice, and cleaving to him; for that means life to you and length of days, that you may dwell in the land which the Lord swore to your fathers, to Abraham, to Isaac, and to Jacob, to give them.

We have a Lord that is sufficient for every hungry soul, and, in return, I believe that every child of God should have the zeal of a zealot. Jesus did not come here to maintain the status quo, and He does not want us to sit and rest easy while the world falls to pieces around us. That is why He said in Matthew 10:34, "Do not think that I have come to bring peace on earth; I have not come to bring peace, but a sword." But He brings about His Kingdom through a revolution of love and truth, one in which, if we love Him, we are called to join. There is no other way, no other truth, no other life. In today's world, you cannot be a Christian and not face confrontation.

This fact means that we must take our gospel message into enemy territory. What does that look like in practice? Well, Jesus said in Matthew 16:18, "And I tell you, you are Peter, and on this rock I will build my church, and the powers of death [also translated as "gates of Hell"] shall not prevail against it [the Church]." Now, look at that sentence again carefully, and take note: gates don't attack. We know that! They are defensive structures, not something active that runs out in a battlefield. This means that it's the Church that's on the move, and the gates of Hell can't stop us. Hell's gates are being "storm rushed" by God's people, and they can't hold us back. When we read this verse from Matthew, I think it's safe to say that most of us usually think that the Lord is promising that the Church, which is His Body, will withstand all the attacks launched *against* it. Of course, that is true. But remember this careful reading of it. It is the Kingdom of God that is launching the attack against the powers of Hell — and it is the gates of Satan that are on the defensive.

What does it mean that we, as God's people, as His Church, are called to take the offensive? It means we have to run into enemy territory and gain ground for Jesus Christ. We can't sit around waiting for an invitation to stand up and go out and do the right thing; we already have a command. It is wise and prudent to make the necessary preparations for such work, but we do not wait for circumstances to be perfect. And besides, we already have the One who has gone before us, who has shown us how it's done. Jesus has given us the ultimate example of what it means to face down the gates of Hell.

One example of this showdown, and one we can join in directly and practically in this day and age, is 40 Days for Life. During each of the 40 Days for Life campaigns, people commit to pray, fast, help their communities, and hold vigils outside of abortion clinics for forty days in order to end abortion. These pro-life warriors storm the gates of death. They show us how, in prayer, which looks peaceful to casual onlookers, we can take the offensive against the culture of death. We push forward, expanding the boundaries of the Kingdom of Christ. And we must keep moving! We know that the gates of Hell will not prevail against this movement, this offensive tactic taken in defense of vulnerable lives. The gates of falsehood on this front of the culture of death flee in the presence of truth — a presence that is fueled and supplied by the power of prayer that releases a shower of graces — and the gates of sin will melt in the presence of that grace. The gates of death will fall in the presence of the Church; they will not prevail in the face of the prayers of the people of life!

Heroic men and women are found in abundance in the pro-life movement. They are true champions of life, totally dedicated to protecting and defending the dignity and sanctity of all innocent human life. They tirelessly and selflessly fight the culture of death, placing themselves in harm's way as they stand on the front lines of abortion clinics and engage the demons of abortion in fierce combat. I stand in awe of them, and I commend them for their great work; and yet they refuse to take credit for their remarkable achievement. Instead, they give God all the glory, as they should.

Nevertheless, in the strife we encounter in such efforts as 40 Days for Life, we are made aware again and again that the devil has taken a lot of territory; running into his chaos hammers home the truth that we have to take that territory back. We have to have the spirit of a soldier, the guts of a gladiator, and the attitude of an athlete. We need to say with St. Paul, "For to me to live is Christ, and to die is gain" (Phil. 1:21). If we can get our heads in that same place, we'll be invincible in all the ways that really matter; what the demons don't realize is that you can't do anything to a man who looks at death as a positive option. And how do we get our heads in that place? Through prayer, of course.

There are many types of prayer, such as: liturgical, vocal, meditative, contemplative, intercessory, imperative, and prayers of supplication. Of these, liturgical prayers are especially powerful. When we pray liturgically, we are mirroring on earth what is constantly happening in Heaven — the worship of God by all the angels and saints. And so, the liturgical prayers of the Church carry the weight of the entire Church Militant, Church Suffering, and Church Triumphant, combining their prayers together in glorious strength.

In this book, I want to focus on prayer as an offensive weapon. Prayer is a weapon that makes us joyful! But it is still a weapon. St. John Chrysostom (347–407 A.D.), a gifted preacher, bishop of Constantinople, and Doctor of the Church, spoke about this power of prayer:

> For prayer is a mighty weapon, an unfailing treasure, a wealth which is never expended, a harbor that is always calm, a foundation for tranquility. Prayer is the root and source and mother of ten thousand blessings. It is more powerful than the empire itself.… I am not talking of a prayer lightly and carelessly offered but of one made in earnest, which comes from an afflicted soul and from a contrite heart. This is the kind of prayer which mounts to Heaven.… The power of prayer quenched the force of fire, it curbed the wrath of lions, it brought an end to wars, it stopped battles, it quelled storms, it drove out demons, it opened the gates of Heaven, it cut asunder the chains of death, it put sickness to flight, it beat off insults and abuse, it made shaken cities stand. Prayer removed blows inflicted from above, it took away the plots and treachery of men, and, in a word, every dread event.[1]

[1] St. John Chrysostom, "Homily 5," *On the Incomprehensible Nature of God,* trans. Paul W. Harkins, in *The Fathers of the Church,* vol. 72 (Washington, D.C.: Catholic University of America Press, 1984), nos. 44, 46, 57.

If Catholic Christians really understood the full extent of the power we have available through prayer, we would be speechless. But where does the offensive power of prayer come from? What does it mean that prayer can be an offensive weapon? To understand these concepts, we need to look to Scripture. When the Holy Bible says to "put on Christ" (see Gal. 3:27), it indicates that we are the heirs of Christ; in this language of inheritance and reception, we know that we are God's sons and daughters. Our *divine* sonship means that we get to take on the rights and privileges of Christ: "We share in Christ" (Heb. 3:14). This sonship, this sharing in Christ, is where we derive our power in prayer. When we walk in "the obedience of faith" (Rom. 1:5; 16:26) and live in friendship with God (James 2:23), we come to know in practice that "the prayer of a righteous man has great power in its effects" (James 5:16).

Many prayers, especially prayers of petition or prayers of intercession, are requests of God. The word *prayer* even comes from the Latin word *prex*, which means "a request." And so, when we pray, we are often asking God to help us in whatever we are facing — or to help whomever it is we are praying for. In response to our requests of Him, He gives our prayers offensive power, and, because we are going to Him, our prayers have the power to prevail against the gates of Hell. As Jesus tells us in Luke 11:11–13, "What father among you, if his son asks for a fish, will instead of a fish give him a serpent; or if he asks for an egg, will give him a scorpion? If you then, who are evil, know how to give good gifts to your children, how much more will the heavenly Father give the Holy Spirit to those who ask him!"

When you were baptized, you became a child of God (John 3:5), and when you were confirmed, you became a soldier of Christ (2 Tim. 2:1–13). When, at your Confirmation, the bishop, a general in the Catholic Church, laid his hands on your head, he gave you a mystical sword, "the sword of the Spirit, which is the word of God"

(Eph. 6:17). Christ our King has entrusted you with this sword to fight the culture of death and to fight the demons that roam the earth and seek the damnation of every man, woman, and child. But though your sword is an offensive weapon, you must be a *joyful* warrior as you slay both errors and demons (see 2 Macc. 15:26–28). When you die, you will kneel before the judgment seat of Christ the King (see 2 Cor. 5:10). Our Lord will look at your sword and inspect it. If He sees that your sword is clean, that it was never used, that it looks exactly the way you received it at your Confirmation — if He sees that you never evangelized, that you were lukewarm, that you were not a prayer warrior — He will say to you, "I never knew you; depart from me, you evildoers" (Matt. 7:23). But, if you have done your job, our Lord will take the sword from your hands as you kneel before Him, and He will see that it's full of scratches: It's dented, it's chipped, it has nicks all over it, and it's colored with the blood of warfare. And then our Lord will say to you, "Well done, good and faithful servant" (Matt. 25:21).

In the end of all things, when we are facing eternity, there will only be winners, and losers. Heaven, and Hell. And we choose our own destinies, right here, right now, by how we choose to live our lives. Will you fill your life with earthly treasures and worldly thoughts, or will you pick up your sword and fill your mind with the Scripture and prayer that will train your hands for warfare? Remember, as you make your decision, that when you leave this world, you'll take nothing of it with you. I don't know about you, but I've never seen a hearse pulling a U-Haul.

## One More Round

Before we move on to the rest of this book, I want to wrap up this Introduction with a story of someone who would not quit, someone who kept staying in for "just one more round." Whenever we feel beaten down in our work of spiritual warfare, this example can inspire us to keep going, to keep moving along in our faith journey, to not give up.

John L. Sullivan was the heavyweight champion of the world in the nineteenth century. On July 7, 1889, when he weighed 212 pounds, he was scheduled to fight a pipsqueak who went by the name of "Gentlemen Jim Corbett" who weighed in at only 178 pounds. The odds were stacked way against this little guy; all the experts said he had a thousand to one chance of beating Sullivan.

Let's look at what happened in the *twenty-one* rounds of their fight:

- First round: Sullivan hit Corbett so hard that his body shook like he was having a seizure. His trainer said to him, "How you doin'?" Corbett said, "Not good, I think he broke my ribs." So his trainer said, "I'm going to stop it." But Corbett said, "No, I need one more round."

- Second round: Sullivan hit Corbett so hard that he lifted him off the ground. His trainer said, "Want me to throw in the towel?" Corbett said, "No, I need one more round."

- Third round: Sullivan hit Corbett so many times in the face that his eyes bruised and swelled shut. So his trainer slit his eyelids and released the blood, then told him, "You gotta quit, you can't continue like this." Corbett: "I need one more round."

- Fourth round: Sullivan went out and knocked him down three times in a single round. Corbett went back to his corner like one big bruise. His trainer said, "That's it, I'm gonna stop it." But Corbett said, "No, one more round."

- Fifth round: Sullivan hit Corbett so hard he thought he was going to die. His trainer said, "I gotta stop it right now." And again, Corbett said, "No, one more round."

✠ This went on until the *twentieth* round: Corbett came out bloody and bludgeoned, eyes puffed, nose and mouth bloody, forehead swollen, legs weak, too tired to stand. He was beaten from ring post to ring post. But even then, when he went back to his corner, he told his trainer, "One more round!"

✠ Twenty-first round: Corbett came out, half dead, to the middle of the ring, threw a right cross left hook flush on Sullivan's jaw — and knocked him out cold.

Children of God, soldiers of Christ, let me tell you something: We have a Sullivan in our midst. His name is the devil, and when he hits you and knocks you down, you gotta get up and say, "One. More. Round." Remember, we've got *Jesus* in our corner. *Jesus* is our trainer. We have nothing to fear. We are in good hands. All you people reading this, you people who are the Church Militant here on earth, don't give up, don't stop, don't quit, just keep going, "fight the good fight of faith" (1 Tim. 6:12). When you feel like throwing in the towel, remember: We are part of TEAM JESUS, and He is an army of ONE. And you, as a Christian, are a warrior of prayer.

In the following chapters, we'll talk through the theology of prayer, how to approach it, and what we need for our prayers to be effective. What does it mean to be a soldier on the battlefield between good and evil in today's world, and how do we arm ourselves with prayer? Then, we'll talk about some particular moments in my life and in the lives of some of my friends and family members where the power of prayer was undeniably a weapon — sometimes offensive, sometimes protective. Next, we'll look at various quotations — from Scripture, the *Catechism of the Catholic Church*, and from various Catholic writers and saints — that teach us how to be prayer warriors. Finally, at the end of the book, you will find an appendix full of prayers to help you pray like a joyful warrior and fight the enemy through your prayers. For God has not called us to a playground, but to a battleground. Through it all, through each section, my mission statement for this book, which I hope you can all adopt and make your own as you read it, is simple: love God, save souls, slay error!

# Understanding Prayer as a Weapon: Prepare for Glory

# CHAPTER 1

# Theology of Prayer

## THE BASICS

ALL CATHOLIC PRAYER COMES explicitly or implicitly from the Word of God. St. Teresa of Ávila tells us that the goal of our life and the goal of prayer is "union with God," and Fr. Cliff Ermatinger, an exorcist from Milwaukee, states simply that "prayer purifies the intellect."[2] With similar simplicity, St. Teresa of Calcutta famously prayed for Jesus to "penetrate and possess my whole being so utterly that all my life may only be a radiance of Thine."[3]

Dr. Dan Schneider, a theologian at Franciscan University of Steubenville, speaks specifically about mental prayer, its offensive and defensive nature, and the way that the power of God, invoked through prayer, combats demonic power: "Mental Prayer gives you custody of the mind or imagination (that's the pre-intellect). Prayer projects those thoughts into the cosmos (heavenly places) — that's its offensive nature — and it also sets up a defensive perimeter. Prayer makes the power of God present. *Anamnesis* is a Greek word that means more than just 'remember'; it makes the prayer 'present.'

---

[2]   Cliff Ermatinger, "The Interior Life" (lecture, Holy Cross Catholic Church, Mesa, AZ, March 4, 2020).

[3]   Philip Kosloski, "Mother Teresa Prayed This Inspirational Prayer on a Daily Basis," *Aleteia* (September 5, 2018), https://aleteia.org/2018/09/05/mother-teresa-prayed-this-inspirational-prayer-on-a-daily-basis.

Demons attack the imagination because they don't want you to pray. Demons traffic through the senses."

In 2 Kings 6:15–18, the Old Testament gives us a perfect example of what it means that prayer is such a concrete weapon against enemies, demonic or otherwise:

> When the servant of the man of God rose early in the morning and went out, behold, an army with horses and chariots was round about the city. And the servant said, "Alas, my master! What shall we do?" He said, "Fear not, for those who are with us are more than those who are with them." Then Eli'sha prayed, and said, "O Lord, I pray thee, open his eyes that he may see." So the Lord opened the eyes of the young man, and he saw; and behold, the mountain was full of horses and chariots of fire round about Eli'sha. And when the Syrians came down against him, Eli'sha prayed to the Lord, and said, "Strike this people, I pray thee, with blindness." So he struck them with blindness in accordance with the prayer of Eli'sha.

In plain language, this is how we can understand this passage:

> The Syrian King goes out with an army to arrest Elisha and so they surround the town of Dothan where the prophet is living. Elisha's servant is terrified, but the prophet prays to the Lord to open the man's eyes spiritually: in an instant he sees the vast heavenly army arrayed in invisible ranks with their chariots of fire ablaze in the sky. Elisha's words enabled his terrified companion to see the divine army protecting the Israelites from their Syrian enemies. Elisha asks the Lord to strike them blind and so he does. This ends Syria's attack upon Israel. So it is with Christians who face death. The devil

will come to tempt them, but their guardian angels will come to strengthen them. Their patron saints and protectors will come also, as well as St. Michael the Archangel whom God has appointed as the defender of his faithful servants at the time of their death. The Blessed Virgin Mary will also come to protect her children who so often prayed to her for help "now and at the hour of our death."[4]

Knowing without a doubt that we are protected in this way because of God's power given in response to our prayers, "Let us seal the doorpost of our inner thoughts with the Protective Word of God, just as the Israelites marked the doorpost of their houses with the saving blood of the Paschal lamb. So we are guarded from every enemy (demons) by constant return to prayer in moments of quiet."[5]

## THE POWERS OF THE SOUL

St. Thomas Aquinas says that the soul of every person is divided primarily into intellective and sensitive faculties: What do we learn and know through our intelligence, our intellect, and what do we learn and know through our senses? When we think about spiritual warfare with the enemy, we realize pretty quickly that we need to know what weapons we have in our arsenal. What powers do we have within these two faculties? Well, each one of those faculties has two parts within it, the cognitive and the appetitive. So all together we have our intellective cognitive faculty, our intellective appetitive faculty, our sensitive cognitive faculty, and our sensitive appetitive faculty. Our *intellect*, how we use our reason to make decisions and logically understand the world around us, is rooted in our intellective cognitive faculty. Our *will*, what we want to do, driven by our rational appetites, is rooted

---

4   "Meditation of the Day," in *Magnificat* 22, no. 6 (August 2020), 26.
5   "Intercessions," in *Magnificat* 22, no. 13 (March 2021).

in the intellectual appetitive faculty. On the other side, we have our *memory* and *instinct,* which, together with our imagination and what you might call common sense, are rooted in the sensitive cognitive faculty. Finally, *emotion* is rooted in the sensitive appetitive faculty of each human soul; you can think of this as "will" of the appetites of the passions instead of the appetites of the intellect.[6]

All together, then, the weapons in our arsenal are intellect, will, memory, instinct, and emotion. When we go out to face the powers of evil in spiritual warfare, we need to keep a watch on our weapons and guard them from demonic interference.

The good news here is that demons don't actually have direct access to all five of these powers. While they can play with our memory, emotions, and instincts, they can't actually directly affect our intellect and will. They can use our emotions, for example, to play with and sometimes overwhelm our intellect, or to persuade our will one way or the other, but they can never directly control intellect and will. What that means is that if we can keep our emotions and appetites in check, demons will have a hard time messing with us where it really counts. And the best way to purify and strengthen the intellect is by studying the dogmas and doctrines — the teachings and laws — of the Catholic Church and by submitting ourselves to their governance.

If we keep demonic interference away from our intellect, it will be properly ordered to honor the will of God. We will want what He wants *because* He wants it. And that will for what He wants is strengthened through … you guessed it! Prayer. One of the best-known verses in the whole Bible talks about this: "Glory to God in the highest; and on earth peace to men of good will" (Luke 2:14, Douay-Rheims). *Good will* means a will that is aligned with God's

---

6  St. Thomas Aquinas, *Summa Theologica* I, q. 78, art. 1.

will, because "no one is good but God alone" (Mark 10:18). If we are men of good will, then we will have peace. And so, if we want a will that is properly ordered to the intellect, a will and an intellect that are properly ordered to know and want the will of God, we need the order and discipline of prayer. What will this life of dedicated prayer do for you? As St. Augustine said, "If you pray well, you will live well. If you live well, you will die well. If you die well, all will be well."

## The Discipline of Prayer in Monasticism and the Liturgy

The way of life in monasteries and convents is ordered around this need for a disciplined prayer life. As laypeople, we can implement this same sort of monastic discipline in our own prayer lives. This doesn't mean that laypeople have a duty to spend as much time in prayer as men and women do in religious life; we have different vocations for a reason. But we can still pray at specific and regular times each day. For example, we can join the communal prayer of the Church by praying the Angelus at 6 a.m., noon, and 6 p.m., or by praying the Liturgy of the Hours — structured and set prayers that are prayed either in whole or in part at particular times of the day. Praying these prayers in union with the whole Church will help us in our conversion to become more like Christ, prompt God to flood us with His grace, snap our lower faculties (memory, emotions, and instinct) back into order, and restore our higher faculties (intellect and will).

St. Benedict, the father of Western monasticism, was one of the first prominent exorcists in the early Catholic Church. He founded monasteries in Italy at a time when the Church was being threatened by pagan Germanic tribes from without and corruption from within. The monasteries were fortresses of prayer, missionary centers among both pagan barbarians and sinful Christians — and prayer was the weapon that converted these evil men, little by little, into faithful Catholic Christians. What does this history have to do with us, today, right here and right now? The discipline of monastic prayer life, adopted and adapted to the needs of individual laymen, effectively turns each person into an individual monastery of prayer. Through a disciplined prayer life, we too can convert and transform the world around us. Pretty powerful stuff.

One of the reasons that monastic prayer is so powerful is that demons fear liturgical prayer, such as the prayers of the Mass or the Liturgy of the Hours, more than any other type of prayer. Why? First, and as we'll learn about later in more detail, demons look for chaos, and they despise order. And liturgical prayer has order in spades. It's got uniformity, structure, and discipline. And it has constancy in its fidelity and its consistency in prayer. Liturgical prayer is the prayer demons used to say in Heaven before their fall; we know this from the Book of Revelation, which says that in Heaven, the saints and angels pray liturgically through acclamations, doxologies, and antiphons (see Rev. 4:8; 4:10–11; 5:11–14; 7:9–12; 19:1–7). Heaven has uniformity and structure, and prayer on earth imitates prayer in Heaven. The Jews prayed liturgically before the coming of Christ, and they still do, which means that our Lord Jesus Christ, who was born and raised in a faithful Jewish family, prayed liturgically. Also, the weight of tradition in liturgical prayer means that all of our prayers are joined together with the whole Church through that tradition and are much stronger because of it. Finally, the liturgy, both in monastic prayer and in the Mass, leans heavily on the Word of God, which is like a sword, an offensive weapon that wounds and torments demons. With all that going for it, no wonder demons are so afraid of liturgical prayer! And so liturgical worship is one of our greatest tools in spiritual warfare.

## Your Focus Matters

Many psychologists and psychiatrists will tell you that when you focus on something, positive or negative, you give it "life and energy." This is as true in the realm of spiritual warfare as it is anywhere else. For example, when you engage in occultist practices, you are in fact conjuring up demons. *Conjure* means to "invoke alongside" by a spell, hex, or curse. It is a command, a "calling upon" something. Just as we invoke the power of God against these demons through prayer, if we are so foolish as to expose ourselves to demonic power through occultist practices, our focus will give them life and negative energy against our own selves — and against the souls of the persons connected to us.

This means that anyone around us who is so foolish as to get himself involved in such demonic activity is also exposing us. And this is another reason why we must pray as though our souls and lives depended on it: the life of your soul *does* depend on it. And there is no better weapon to fight back than prayer; bullets project from the barrel of a gun, and likewise, prayers initiate from your soul and are projected from your mind and your mouth. Pray, pray, pray — even though you get distracted, even though you get sleepy, even though you get no consolation, even though you feel bored. Grind it out. Fight through it. A man who prays is practicing "smashmouth Catholicism," to quote my friend Dr. Dan Schneider (Army Desert Storm veteran). What does that mean? *Smashmouth* is a style of football characterized by a rough, aggressive, hard-hitting, powerful confrontational offensive running game, not relying on skill but on brute force. It doesn't matter that a man's prayers may not sound like cloistered Carmelites singing sacred polyphonic music in an oratory; they can still "destroy [demonic] strongholds" (2 Cor. 10:4). Our prayers beget what they signify — they have an offensive nature to them. And if you need a shot in the arm to remember what smashmouth Catholicism looks like, Ven. Mary Magdalen of Jesus, C.P., wrote: "Now do with me as King Nebuchadnezzar did with the three children. Cast me into the furnace of divine love so that in the midst of the flames I can intone the most perfect praise to God."[7]

## Dolphins and Water

Sacred Scripture demonstrates that animals were given to us by God to teach us something about our ourselves and about our relationship with Him:

> Scripture likewise recognizes a close analogy between human beings and animals. In the old covenant sacrificial system, animals like bulls and goats could stand in as substitutes for humans. Animals can represent humans symbolically, either positively or negatively. Think of Jesus as the "lion of Judah," or the Pharisees as a "brood of vipers," or God's people mounting up "on wings like eagles," etc. There are many more examples throughout Scripture. Animals can serve as illustrations of industriousness (Prov. 6:6–11), loyalty (Isa. 1:3), bondage to folly (2 Pet. 2:22), or even as symbols of whole nations (Dan. 7). And God's people are regularly called a "flock." Indeed, it seems that one reason God created animals was to teach us about ourselves and about Him.[8]

7   Mary Magdalen of Jesus, "Meditation of the Day," in *Magnificat* 24, no. 1 (April 2022), 314.

8   Daniel Hoffman, "What Does the Bible Teach about Animals?" *Knowing Scripture*, March 13, 2018, https://knowingscripture.com/articles/what-does-the-bible-teach-about-animals.

Let's think about dolphins to help us learn about prayer. In early Christianity, dolphins became a symbol of Jesus Christ, who is our lifesaver and who delivers us out of the chaos of this world and onto the shores of Heaven. Dolphins project sound not only to communicate but also to navigate, hunt their prey, and avoid danger through echolocation.[9] This use of sound waves has the same effect as Catholic prayer: just like dolphins use sound to help them navigate through the water, prayer is the way we navigate through this world of sin (see Ps. 119:105, NABRE, "Your word is a lamp for my feet, a light for my path"). Also, just like dolphins use sound to communicate with each other, prayer is the way we communicate with God (see Jer. 29:12, "Then you will call upon me and come and pray to me, and I will hear you"). And finally, just like dolphins use sound as protection against potential threats, our prayer torments and drives out the diabolical. Remember: prayer is a weapon system. When you're about to pray, your system is on the "weapons hot" setting. Focus like a laser, and fire away.

We can also look to other elements in nature to help us understand and appreciate the value of prayer. For instance, Dr. Masaru Emoto, a Japanese scientist, studied how ideas and sounds affect the molecular structure of water. In his book, *The Hidden Messages in Water*, Dr. Emoto tries to prove that positive ideas, such as love and compassion, could change the molecular shape of water into beautiful patterns, while negative ideas, such as fear and hatred, could cause water molecules to form into disfigured shapes and patterns. He took photographs of water molecules exposed either to written words or prayers to demonstrate how they changed in response to whatever human feeling they were exposed to, and he

---

[9]　"Communication and Echolocation," *United Parks and Resorts*, https://seaworld.org/animals/all-about/bottlenose-dolphin/communication/.

saw that water responded to different human ideas. He even looked at the molecules of polluted and toxic water and noticed that they began to resemble in shape and form the molecules of clean, healthy water after they were exposed to prayer or positive ideas.[10]

His work makes us wonder: If words, intentions, and prayer can affect *water*, how much more can they affect human beings, who are a union of physical matter and spiritual soul, created in the image of God?

We know that words have power, especially words of prayer. As Proverbs 18:21 tells us, "Death and life are in the power of the tongue, and those who love it will eat its fruits." And when we look at the life and words of our Lord in the New Testament, we see how His words especially hold power over nature, life, and death. For example, when Jesus "cursed" the fig tree, it died instantly (see Matt. 21:18–19). The word of Jesus even brought Lazarus back from the dead (see John 11:1–44).

Our prayer has incredible power. Rational thought and our ability to speak are part of what separates us from animals. If an animal gets possessed by a demon, there is nothing it can do about it because animals have no rational thought, and they can't speak or think in order to pray. And if a house or toy or other object gets infested by demons, there is nothing it can do because it's inanimate and non-sentient and cannot speak or pray for itself. But we humans can be aware. We can think. We can know. And this means, we can pray. What a gift it is, this ability to pray.

## Big Guns

If you really want to pull out the big guns against evil, prayer needs some companions in the battle. What sort of tools can we add to our prayers to strengthen them?

---

[10] "Dr. Masaru Emoto and Water Consciousness," *The Wellness Enterprise,* March 23, 2017, https://thewellnessenterprise.com/emoto/.

Jesus says that some demons can only be driven out by "prayer and fasting" (see Mark 9:29). Fasting is a sign of discipline, and it shows our fidelity to God. Fasting makes us stronger in prayer because it shows us how much we are dependent on God. While prayer connects us to God, fasting disconnects us from the world. In short, when it is added to prayer, fasting is a "force multiplier," something that increases the effect of a force, such as weapons or other hardware — something that gives a person or military unit the ability to accomplish greater feats than could be accomplished without it.

Most Catholic prayer is comparable to small arms and light weapons (SALW), which refers to portable weapons used by individual infantrymen. SALW are very effective, especially when used by many infantrymen standing side by side, united against the enemy. Kicking it up a notch, Catholic deliverance prayers — prayers that are specifically and directly anti-demonic — are like heavy artillery military weapons, built to launch munitions far beyond the range and power of infantry firearms and to breach defensive walls and fortifications during sieges. Heavy artillery weapons also have a high flash radius, which means they can be seen from far away. Likewise, Catholic deliverance prayers have a high flash radius: they make big impression and have a strong effect against demons and their activities.

Some deliverance prayers, i.e., simple or minor forms of exorcism, are safe for the laity to pray, but some should only be undertaken by priests who, by their grace of state as priests, have the spiritual authority to take on demons in a direct and high-stakes confrontation. Most of us don't have that authority, and *must not attempt to wield it*. Noted exorcist Fr. Chad Ripperger has put together a book of prayers that are safe for the laity to pray: *Deliverance Prayers for Use by the Laity*. If you want to learn more about which deliverance prayers are safe for lay people to pray, you can also look to the USCCB: "Simple or minor forms of exorcism are found in two places: first, for those preparing for

Baptism, the Rite of Christian Initiation of Adults (RCIA) and the Rite of Baptism for Children both call for minor exorcisms; secondly, the appendix of *Exorcisms and Related Supplications* includes a series of prayers which may be used by the faithful."[11]

Major exorcisms, on the other hand, are like carpet bombing, or saturation bombing, which is when a large area is bombed in a progressive manner to inflict damage on every inch of it. This is what a major exorcism does to demons. And again, the USCCB give us a good definition: "The second kind [of exorcism] is the solemn or 'major exorcism,' which is a rite that can only be performed by a bishop or a by priest, with the special and express permission of the local ordinary (cf. Code of Canon Law, can. 1172). This form is directed 'at the expulsion of demons or to the liberation [of a person] from demonic possession' (Catechism of the Catholic Church, no. 1673)."[12] These extremely powerful prayers are not to be prayed by laypeople, though we can assist the Church by uniting our prayers to her and by praying for our priests.

## Main Take-Aways

If our prayers are not answered, it is because, as St. James says, "you ask wrongly, to spend it on your passions" (James 4:3). Beyond the obvious here — that we need to be asking for the right things and not just the things that our passions prompt us to — there are three conditions we need to keep in mind as we move to pray.

First, we have to pray with humility: "My sacrifice, O God, is a contrite spirit; a contrite, humbled heart, O God, you will not scorn" (Ps. 51:19, NABRE). It doesn't matter if someone is a saint or sinner; God hears those who are humble. Anyone who comes forward with

---

[11]  "Exorcism," *United States Conference of Catholic Bishops,* https://www.usccb.org/prayer-and-worship/sacraments-and-sacramentals/sacramentals-blessings/exorcism.

[12]  Ibid.

an attitude of resentment, entitlement, hubris, or pride, or anyone who is centered on himself, is not going to be praying an efficacious prayer. In their pride, these people attribute qualities to themselves that belong to God. That is why Scripture says, "God opposes the proud, but gives grace to the humble" (James 4:6). But if we come to God with humility, He will say to us, "I have heard your prayer; I have seen your tears. Now I am healing you" (2 Kings 20:5, NABRE).

A second condition for effective prayer is confidence, which is the unconditional hope of obtaining all that is helpful toward salvation. In teaching the Our Father, Christ taught His disciples to approach God with the confidence of a child to a parent. People who have confidence believe that God will keep the promises that Jesus was speaking about when He said, "Whatever you ask the Father in my name he will give you" (John 16:23, NABRE). Indeed, St. Augustine says, "For God has made Himself a debtor … not by borrowing; but by promising."[13]

The last condition for effective prayer that I want to address right now is perseverance. God wishes to unite Himself to those who "pray constantly" (1 Thess. 5:17). Christ tells His disciples that it is not sufficient simply to ask; we must insist. Jesus says, "seek and you will find, knock, and it will be opened to you" (Luke 11:9). Persevering in prayer will result in obtaining what you ask for beyond expectations. As St. Bernard says, "Let no one undervalue his prayer, for God does not undervalue it.… He will give either what we ask, or what He knows to be better."[14]

---

[13] St. Augustine, trans. by R. G. MacMullen, "Sermon 60 on the New Testament," in *Nicene and Post-Nicene Fathers*, first series, vol. 6, ed. by Philip Schaff (Buffalo, NY: Christian Literature Publishing, 1888.), no. 4.

[14] St. Bernard, "*De Quad.*, serm. 5," quoted in St. Alphonsus de Liguori, *The Great Means of Salvation and of Perfection*, ed. Eugene Grimm (New York: Aeterna Press, 2015).

# Chapter 2

# A Dedicated Life of Prayer Takes Humility

St. Augustine said that the three greatest virtues are "humility, humility, and humility."[15] Humility is the true and first weapon of spiritual warfare. Satan and the other rebellious angels fell because of their pride, and just as pride was the beginning of evil in the world, so is humility the first building block of retaking the world for good, of kicking evil to the curb. When we give in to sinful pride, we are imitating, to one degree or another, those demons who first rebelled against God. But Jesus makes clear to us by His life and death that there is real spiritual power in humility, which is why the devil and his demons detest it so much. They fear those who strive for and who live out the virtue of humility in their daily lives.

The shortest and clearest definition of humility that I have ever heard is from St. Thérèse of Lisieux, who said, "It appears to me that humility is the truth."[16] And what is the truth? The truth is that we were created to know, love, and serve God in this world and to be happy with Him forever in the next.[17] This truth enrages the devil

---

15   See St. Augustine, letter 118, no. 22.

16   St. Thérèse of Lisieux, *Thoughts of Saint Thérèse of the Child Jesus*, trans. an Irish Carmelite (New York: P. J. Kenedy and Sons, 1915).

17   *Baltimore Catechism*, no. 1, q. 6.

and his demons. They are about "my own will be done"; they do not want the will of God to be done. And they absolutely do not want us to do God's will either, so they try to trip us up by provoking us to battle against humility. What can we do in the face of this attack? Seek to know, love, and serve God daily, and strive to be a humble servant to those around us. A real practice of humility will drive the enemy right back in powerful ways, since humility is the one thing the enemy cannot imitate, and we will learn in practice the truth of what Scripture tells us: "When pride comes, then comes disgrace; but with the humble is wisdom" (Prov. 11:2).

Humility is the one virtue that underlies every other virtue, and, as we have discussed, it has a unique power to counter and conquer Satan's pride. Fasting goes hand in hand with humility in defeating the devil, because through the mortification of our flesh and bodily needs, we learn how to rely on God and control our passionate wants. Together, then, humility and fasting are the two great weapons against Satan in the spiritual battle we face.

Fasting is pretty straightforward, even if it isn't easy, but how do you increase your humility? First and always, pray for it. God will always find ways to increase your humility if you ask Him for it. It's likely that these ways won't be too enjoyable on a human level, but you'll know that whatever happens is good for you! One way to pray for humility is to say the *Litany of Humility*, which was written by Cardinal Merry del Val (d. 1930), the secretary of state for Pope St. Pius X. This prayer, which can be found in the appendix to this book, is a powerful tool that will strengthen our interior disposition, encourage us to pray, and grant us willingness to suffer so that we may be true and steadfast soldiers for Christ.

Humility is the virtue that is typical of all the saints, the one virtue that underlies every other virtue, and without which none of us will enter Heaven. Fill yourself with humility, and you will soon find that all other virtues will easily build on it — and the devil won't know what's hit him. As one popular saying goes: One day, the devil saw me with my head down. He thought he'd won. He thought I was defeated. But then, as I lifted up my head, he heard me say, "Amen."

Let's continue to think about humility, using these three passages from Scripture as we meditate on it and try to give ourselves over to it. The first two are in Jesus' own words from the Gospel of Matthew, and the third is from St. Paul's Letter to the Philippians:

✠ "Learn from me; for I am gentle and lowly [humble] in heart" (Matt. 11:29).

✠ "Truly, I say to you, unless you turn and become like children, you will never enter the kingdom of heaven" (Matt. 18:3).

✠ "Do nothing from selfishness or conceit, but in humility count others better than yourselves. Let each of you look not only to his own interests, but also to the interests of others. Have this mind among yourselves, which was in Christ Jesus, who, though he was in the form of God, did not count equality with God a thing to be grasped, but emptied himself, taking the form of a servant, being born in the likeness of men. And being found in human form he humbled himself and became obedient unto death, even death on a cross. Therefore God has highly exalted him and bestowed on him the name which is above every name" (Phil. 2:3–9).

# Chapter 3

# Through Our Prayers, Angels Fight Demons for Us

Demons are attracted to faithlessness, disorder, and the unclean. Warning of their ability to get to us when we are not disciplined, not paying attention, and not being vigilant in our watch against them, noted exorcist Fr. Chad Ripperger says, "Angels come wherever they are called, demons come wherever they are not resisted."[18] On this same subject of parallel distinctions between angels and demons, Fr. David Nix cautions, "When you say the name of Jesus in prayer, angels come to you and demons flee. When you misuse the name of Jesus, angels flee and demons come to you."[19]

Demons are real, and they are here. But God has not abandoned us to fight them on our own. Rather, He has given us His host of

---

[18]   Kyle Clement, who works with Fr. Ripperger, shared the following with me in a personal email, dated November 2, 2020: "Jesse, This is a phrase I first used in 2007 for a presentation at the Pope Leo XIII Institute describing the difference in an Angelic paradigm and a demonic paradigm. These concepts and the quote were part of the first team training presentation I gave in Dan's Diocese of Las Cruces, New Mexico. You both may use it. +JMJ+ Kyle Clement."

[19]   Fr. David Nix, "15 Mortal Sins Catholics Are Missing in Their Confessions," *Pilgrim Priest*, August 3, 2019, https://padreperegrino.org/2019/08/mortalsins/.

angels to fight with and for us. One incredible contemporary example of angels battling demons in defense of faithful Christians is when Boko Haram, a terrorist organization, was about to execute seventy-two Nigerian Christians by firing squad — and angels intervened. The terrorists had their rifles cocked and were preparing to take aim at the persecuted Christians, but suddenly they threw their weapons down and started violently grabbing at their own heads, screaming and shouting that they were covered with snakes. Some of them ran away, but others dropped dead where they stood.

One of the dying terrorists dropped his gun, and a Christian captive reached down to grab it, hoping to shoot at the fleeing Boko Haram militants and help the Christians escape, but the youngest child put her hand on his arm to stop him. "You don't need to do that," she said. "Can you not see the men in white fighting for us?"

All seventy-two captives survived and escaped.[20]

What was happening in this instance? Demons were at work in the actions of the terrorist, ready to kill these Christians, even the little children, because of their faith. But just as the demons were present, so too, because of the faith and prayers of these Christians, were the angels present.

Fr. Ripperger warns of the constant dichotomy, the constant warring, between angelic and demonic forces: "Just as we have guardian angels assigned to us ... Satan may likewise assign a demon, often to an entire family. Lesser demons are sent to tempt and open the door to higher demonic realms."[21] *God gives us our guardian angels*

---

[20] "God's Intervention Saves 72 Captive Nigerian Christians from Boko Haram Firing Squad," *Barnabas Aid*, March 19, 2019, https://www.barnabasaid.org/us/news/god-s-intervention-saves-72-captive-nigerian-christians-from-boko-haram/.

[21] "Archives: Exorcist on Generational Healing," *Spirit Daily*, December 23, 2017, https://spiritdaily.org/blog/spiritual-warfare/exorcist-on-generational-healing.

*for many reasons, chief among them to ward off demons.* Sometimes we visualize moral decision-making as a debate between a bad angel whispering in one ear and a good angel speaking wisely in the other, and there is a certain truth to this: according to St. Thomas Aquinas, one of the roles of the guardian angels is to fight off demons.[22] St. John Bosco also speaks to this conflict and advises us to be bold in asking our angels for help: "When tempted, invoke your Angel. He is more eager to help you than you are to be helped! . . . Ignore the devil and do not be afraid of him: he trembles and flees at your Guardian Angel's sight."[23] And as stated in the *Baltimore Catechism*, "Our guardian angels pray for us, protect and guide us, and offer our prayers, good works and desires to God."[24]

[22]  St. Thomas Aquinas, *Summa Theologica* I, q. 113, arts. 2–6.
[23]  Giovanni Battista Lemoyne, S.D.B., *The Biographical Memoirs of Saint John Bosco*, vol. 2, trans. Felix J. Penna, ed. Diego Borgatello (New Rochelle, NY: Salesiana Publishers, 1966), 205.
[24]  *Baltimore Catechism*, no. 3, q. 223.

# CHAPTER 4

# Prayer Increases Order and Fights Disorder

FR. EDWARD BROOM, O.M.V., writes:

Prayer is meant to order our disorders. As a result of the Original Sin that we all inherit in the moment of our conception, our life is marked with disorder. Our thought process, our will, our emotional state of being, our soul, our intentions, our family and social life — all have a certain disorder. St. Ignatius of Loyola suggests that we do the Spiritual Exercises so as to order the disordered in our lives. Sin causes disorder; prayer brings order. Prayer to Our Lady communicates to our soul and lives the Holy Spirit and the Holy Spirit is a God of order. Our Lady of Guadalupe with her own hands ordered the roses in the tilma of St. Juan Diego. By praying the most holy Rosary, Our Lady can help to order the disordered in our lives.... Another wonderful effect of praying the most Holy Rosary is peace of mind, heart, and soul. We all desire peace, and Our Lady of the Rosary, also known with the title "Queen of Peace," can definitely attain for us this peace that our hearts so ardently yearn. St. Augustine defines peace as the tranquility of order. As the hymn reminds us: "Let there be peace on earth and let it begin with me."[25]

Our souls long for order, and we must pray to combat the disorder in our own lives as well as in the world around us.

Our culture is steeped in disorder. For example, one of the two major parties in our electoral system, the Democratic Party, tragically supports two inherently evil issues that involve disorder. First, the LGBTQ agenda, especially the idea that one can choose his or her own gender and the redefining of marriage to include same sex "marriages," is an inherently disordered system of belief with disastrous social effects. The second disordered platform is closely linked to this first: the idea of the "right" to an abortion is an attack on the fruit of marriage and a contradiction to the scriptural blessing to "be fruitful and multiply, and fill the earth" (Gen. 1:28). The vicious satanic attack and murder of unborn babies in the womb represents a complete disorder of the natural order, the natural good. If we cannot understand this through the natural law, we can know it because God commanded the multiplication of life; it is in rebellion against this commandment, that is, it is in sin, that man chooses to destroy life and defiantly violate God's commandment, "You shall not kill" (Exod. 20:13).

Because the family, the basic building block of society, has been so directly attacked in recent decades, it should be no surprise to us that we are witnessing our culture literally falling apart. Pope St. John Paul II famously wrote, "God in His deepest mystery is not a solitude, but a family, since He has in Himself Fatherhood,

---

[25] Fr. Edward Broom, O.M.V., "Ten Reasons to Start Praying the Rosary," *Catholic Exchange,* October 13, 2020, https://catholicexchange.com/ten-reasons-to-pray-the-holy-rosary/.

Sonship, and the essence of the family, which is love."[26] An attack on the family, then, which is built in the image of God in the Trinity, is an attack on God Himself. No doubt this is why Sr. Lucia, the only one of the three Fatima visionaries who survived to adulthood, wrote in one of her letters to Cardinal Carlo Caffarra: "The final battle between the Lord and the kingdom of Satan will be about Marriage and the Family. Don't be afraid, because whoever works for the sanctity of Marriage and the Family will always be fought against and opposed in every way, because this is the decisive issue."[27]

As we are thinking about this war between order and disorder, notice the primary prayer in Catholic worship is called "The *Order* of the Mass." We can juxtapose this idea with the disorder of the Black Mass, the ultimate form of sacrilege and mockery. Similarly, our Catholic clergy's vocation is called Holy Orders; meanwhile the satanic priests have "unholy orders."

We can take hope, however, in the fact that this disorder is ultimately self-defeating, for, as the saying goes, demons militate to absurdity. The order of society has come crumbling down with alarming, relentless, and dizzying implosion. But the new "norms" that society is embracing will keep getting more and more absurd because the devil cannot bridle his desires. As things are pushed into such bizarre chaos that human reason can't help but start recognizing it for the chaos that it is, people will finally start to resist and push back. Demonic lust for disorder is insatiable, but it will

---

[26] Pope St. John Paul II, Homily, Puebla de Los Angeles, Mexico (January 28, 1979).

[27] CNA Staff, "Fatima Visionary Predicted 'Final Battle' Would Be over Marriage, Family," *Catholic News Agency*, October 13, 2021, https://www.catholicnewsagency.com/news/34155/fatima-visionary-predicted-final-battle-would-be-over-marriage-family.

defeat itself. And as we start to push back against the disorder, we will see in practice that demons fear and flee from the imposition of order as much as they do our prayers themselves.

# Prayer Should Be Specific: Ask for What You Want

Scripture tells us clearly that we ought to be specific when we pray, that we should ask God for what we want. In the Old Testament, for example, in the story of Solomon, we see God giving Solomon this instruction in a dream: "In Gibeon the Lord appeared to Solomon in a dream at night. God said: Whatever you ask I shall give you. Solomon answered.... Give your servant, therefore, a listening heart to judge your people and to distinguish between good and evil.... The Lord was pleased by Solomon's request. So God said to him ... I now do as you request" (1 Kings 3:5–6, 9–12, NABRE).

Again, in the New Testament, in the Gospel of Matthew, our Lord reaffirms this message: "Ask and it will be given to you; seek and you will find; knock and the door will be opened to you. For everyone who asks, receives; and the one who seeks, finds; and to the one who knocks, the door will be opened" (7:7–8, NABRE). And, in the Gospel of John, Jesus commands us to "ask" in prayer no fewer than nine times! Supplication and petitionary prayer do not just come from our personal needs. The Lord *wants* us to ask Him for certain things, and Sacred Scripture tells us what the Lord wishes us to pray for.

It is not only in Scripture that our Lord tells us that He wants to hear the smallest concerns and desires of our hearts. As we read from His revelations to St. Faustina in her diary:

> Today, the Lord said to me, "My daughter, I am told that there is much simplicity in you, so why not tell Me about everything that concerns you, even the smallest details? Tell Me about everything, and know that this will give Me great joy." I answered, "But You know about everything, Lord." And Jesus replied to me, "Yes, I do know; but you should not excuse yourself with the fact that I know, but with childlike simplicity talk to Me about everything, for My ears and heart are inclined towards you, and your words are dear Me."[28]

We will learn about sacramentals in more detail later, but, in our current context of asking for what we want in prayer, I do want to mention some details about the Miraculous Medal right now. The images on the Miraculous Medal were designed by the Blessed Mother herself as she described them to St. Catherine Labouré. In the image on the medal, some of Our Blessed Mother's fingers have rays coming from them. Our Lady told St. Catherine that these rays represent the graces that God gives us if only we *ask* for them and are open to them. But some of her fingers do not have any rays coming from them. Our Lady told St. Catherine that these empty fingers represent the graces not given because we never ask for them. In other words, God will grant us infinite blessings and graces if only we ask; we only limit ourselves by *not asking*. And so, through the image of the Miraculous Medal, Mary, as always,

---

[28]   St. Maria Faustina Kowalska, *Diary* (Stockbridge, MA: Marian Press, 2005), no. 921.

echoes the truth of her Son, who promises us, "Ask, and it will be given you" (Matt. 7:7).[29]

Dr. Dan Schneider and Kyle Clement, who are instructors of Catholic healing, deliverance, and exorcism, add more to the idea of praying for what we want: "When you pray, you get what you ask for. Prayer has an effect; it begets what you ask for. Demons respond to 1. authority, 2. the merit of your prayer (state of grace, purity of life), 3. precision of the prayer (prayer begets what it signifies)." They tell us not only that we should pray for what we desire, but also that our prayers can only be *ideally* effective when we are praying in a state of grace. This is not to say that our prayers cannot be at all effective if we are not in a state of grace (think, for example, of the Good Thief, the Prodigal Son, or any repentant sinner), but that our prayers have the most potential to effect the most grace when we are coming from a place of strength —when we are already in a state of grace. "To him who has will more be given" (Matt. 13-12).

As a sidenote, on this last point, it is worth mentioning that, while exorcists are given the authority to perform major exorcisms by their bishops, each priest prepares on his own for days for each particular exorcism session, primarily by living in a state of grace. Strengthened and enabled by this state of grace, the priest's prayers, when he moves into direct combat on the day of exorcism, will be primed to be precision weapons, perfectly formulated to torment and drive out the demon from the afflicted person. Msgr. Stephen Rosetti address this as well: "I have learned much about the practice of our faith in the course of being an exorcist … how to pray most effectively: I need to slow down, and say the prayers, including the Rite of Exorcism, thoughtfully and deliberately. It makes a

---

[29]  Amy Brooks, "5 Reasons Why I Wear a Miraculous Medal — snd Why You Should Try It Too!" *Church Pop*, March 3, 2016, https://www.churchpop.com/5-reasons-wear-miraculous-medal/.

difference."[30] As the laity, we should learn from this priestly example; while we do not have the spiritual authority of priests, do not possess the grace of their state to take on the spiritual battles that they are trained and charged with waging for us, we each have our own objectively lower-stakes battles that we have to be prepared to fight every day. Like our exorcist priests, we need to keep ourselves in tip-top spiritual fighting form, doing our reps and exercises every day that will keep us ready for the fight whenever the newest demonic challenge rears its ugly head at us. Our regular and daily prayers will build us up spiritually so that we're ready for each new battle and so that we're able to ask for what we need, for the desires of our hearts.

One last story to reflect on as you think about preparing yourself for prayer and being bold enough to ask for what you want: Diego, an eight-year-old boy in Mexico, had such strong faith in the Blessed Sacrament that he transformed his family. Diego's father was not only an alcoholic but also abusive; because of his vices, their whole family lived in a constant state of poverty. Diego started going to adoration at three o'clock in the morning, hoping that his devotion would strengthen his prayers for his father to stop drinking and for his family to escape poverty. Soon, his parents began to accompany him and to pray with him. After a month of family prayer in front of the Eucharist, the father fell back in love with his wife, stopped drinking, and ceased his abuse. Soon after, the family was able to reach a level of financial security. The entire family was healed, and it all began with the humble and persevering faith of an eight-year-old child.[31]

---

[30] Msgr. Stephen Rosetti, "Exorcist Diary #208: Demons 'Teach' Us about Prayer," *Catholic Exorcism*, September 26, 2022, https://www.catholicexorcism.org/post/exorcist-diary-208-demons-teach-us-about-prayer.

[31] Raphael Benedict, "8-Year-Old Prays to the Blessed Sacrament, Obtains Healing for His Family," *Catholic Say*, October 27, 2019, https://catholicsay.com/eight-year-old-boy-prays-to-the-blessed-sacrament-obtains-healing-for-his-family/.

# Chapter 6

# Prayers That Hurt, Wound, and Torment Demons

## Mary and the Rosary

Fr. Gabriele Amorth, who was the exorcist for the diocese of Rome, writes: "One day a colleague of mine heard the devil say during an exorcism, 'Every Hail Mary is like a blow on my head. If Christians knew how powerful the Rosary was, it would be my end.' Anyone who goes to Mary and prays the Rosary cannot be touched by Satan."[32] The reason that the Rosary is so effective is that it is both a prayer directed to the Blessed Virgin and the Holy Trinity and a meditation centered on the life of Jesus and Mary.[33] This sort of meditation carries with it immense spiritual benefits. As St. Isaiah the Hermit, who lived in the fifth century, wrote: "Meditation melts our evil thoughts and withers the passions of the soul; it enlightens our mind, makes the understanding radiant, and fills the heart with joy. Meditation wounds demons and drives away thoughts of wickedness."[34]

With this in mind, all of us Soldiers of Christ, assigned as foot soldiers in the ranks of the Church Militant in our Confirmations, need to

[32]  Fr. Gabriele Amorth, "Exorcism — the Devil — the Rosary," *Our Mother Queen of Peace Times* 21, no. 194 (January–February 2009), 1–2.
[33]  Ibid.
[34]  St. Isaiah the Hermit, in *Magnificat*, vol. 16, no. 7 (September 2014), 5.

get down on our knees and pray the Rosary. Rosary beads are the "beads for the battle," and they train us to a life of discipline, dedication, and concentration. These are the traits of a soldier of Christ. I have never known a champion in boxing, wrestling, or mixed martial arts who did not incorporate hard work every day as part of his training. Prayer, too, is training. The Rosary may be hard work, but we need to grind it out.

Fr. Francesco Bamonte, who succeeded Fr. Gabriele Amorth as the exorcist of Rome, shared the following story: "I took a rosary out and the demon said, 'You are hurting me with those little beads.' I ordered him to answer, 'Why do those beads bother you so much?' And the demon said, 'Why do you hit me so many times? Stop that! Have I not had enough?' With these words I put the rosary on the possessed person and the demon screamed, 'It is heavy, it is crushing me, take it off it is crushing me. You are crushing me! My guts are coming out. Don't you see?"

And now we return to the scene of the Nigerian Christians who were being persecuted by Boko Haram. One of their shepherds was Nigerian bishop Oliver Dashe Doeme, head of the diocese of Maiduguri. In December of 2014, he was in his chapel, praying before the Blessed Sacrament, when he received a vision of our Lord. In this vision, our Lord made it clear that the Islamist militants plaguing Nigeria would be crushed through the Rosary. Bishop Doeme recounted that Jesus appeared before him, holding a sword, and offered it to him in silence. Humbled and surprised, he accepted the sword. As it touched his hands, the sword turned into a Rosary, at which time our Lord and the Rosary both disappeared. Bishop Doeme heard our Lord say three times, "Boko Haram is gone." The bishop recalls, "I didn't need any prophet to give me the explanation. It was clear that with the Rosary, we would be able to expel Boko Haram."[35]

---

[35] Steve Skojec, "Did Jesus Tell This Bishop How to Defeat Boko Haram?" *One Peter Five* (April 22, 2015), https://onepeterfive.com/did-jesus-tell-this-bishop-how-to-defeat-boko-haram/.

There are countless such stories of the power of the Rosary. We could fill an untold number of books with them, but, for our purposes here, before we move on to talk about additional weapons in the arsenal, here are a few more accounts and confirmations for you to chew on:

- ✠ "It is believed that a miracle occurred when St. Dominic placed a rosary over a possessed man's neck: thousands of demons were expelled."[36]

- ✠ "The Holy Rosary is one of the most powerful devotions for the salvation of souls and one of the greatest weapons against the powers of darkness. Bl. Alan exorcised a girl by putting a rosary around her neck and ordered the demons to leave, and they did forthwith."[37]

- ✠ Servant of God Fr. Dolindo Ruotolo (St. Padre Pio's spiritual director) wrote: "The decades of the Rosary are like the belt of a machine gun, every bead is a shot, every affection of the soul is an explosion of faith that frightens off Satan, and Mary once more crushes his head."[38]

- ✠ Fr. Brendan Kilcoyne, Diocese of Tuam, Ireland: "The Rosary is a machine gun of theology. It is where you pepper Hell with the name of God."[39]

---

[36] Donna-Marie Cooper O'Boyle, "Pray the Rosary to Heal a Troubled World," *Catholic Exchange*, November 23, 2020, https://catholicexchange.com/pray-the-rosary-to-heal-a-troubled-world/.

[37] Staff Author, *Stories of Our Blessed Mother* (Hanover, PA: America Needs Fatima, 2003), 29–30.

[38] Fr. Donald Calloway, *Champions of the Rosary* (Stockbridge, MA: Marian Press, 2016), 282.

[39] Fr. Brendan Kilcoyne, "Itinerary: Machine Gun of Theology," episode 032 of *The Brendan Option*, July 14, 2021, produced by Immaculata Productions, YouTube video, 23:03, https://www.youtube.com/watch?v=F9OjRSscDs4&ab_channel=ImmaculataProductions.

✠ Fr. Richard Heilman, Diocese of Madison, Wisconsin: "St. Paul reminds us, 'The weapons we fight with are not the weapons of the world. On the contrary, they have divine power to demolish strongholds' (2 Cor. 10:4). Yes, a divine power is available to all those who choose to enlist in God's army of spiritual warriors, ready to stand 'God Strong' against evil's clear and present danger. 'Go Weapons Hot' is a military command that means to make whatever preparations are necessary so that when you pull the trigger, something happens. In spiritual terms, are we using live ammunition, or are we firing blanks? In other words, are we making the preparations necessary to ensure that our efforts to combat evil and rescue souls are ignited by the fire of the Holy Spirit? As a commissioned officer in the Church Militant, am I imploring God to supernaturally weaponize my prayers (priest), words (prophet), and deeds (king) so that 'I can do all things through Christ Who gives me strength' (Phil. 4:13)? Or am I ignoring His supernatural strength and power and, therefore, firing blanks?"[40]

It is not just the Rosary itself; demons are terrified of anything connected to the Blessed Mother. Fr. Gabriele Amorth writes in his book, *An Exorcist Explains the Demonic*:

> The demon is terrified of her. In order to be very clear, I wish to cite an episode at which I personally assisted many years ago. During an exorcism, [Servant of God] Father Candido [Amantini] asked the devil a question: "Why are you more afraid when I invoke Mary than when I implore God Himself?" He [the devil] responded: "I

---

[40] Fr. Richard Heilman, "Spiritual Warfare: Go Weapons Hot!," *OnePeter-Five*, August 25, 2014, https://onepeterfive.com/spiritual-warfare-go-weapons-hot/.

feel more humiliated being conquered by a simple creature than by God Himself."[41]

## THE NAME OF JESUS AND THE SIGN OF THE CROSS

In addition to the Rosary and any invocation of Mary, we know well that the sign of the cross and speaking the Name of Jesus Christ both put demons to flight. St. Athanasius (c. 296–373 A.D.) explains:

> These things which we have said are no mere words: they are attested by actual experience. Anyone who likes may see the proof of glory in the virgins of Christ, and in the young men who practice chastity as part of their religion, and in the assurance of immortality in so great and glad a company of martyrs. Anyone, too, may put what we have said to the proof of experience in another way. In the very presence of the fraud of demons and the imposture of the oracles and the wonders of magic, let him use the sign of the cross which they all mock at, and but speak the Name of Christ, and he shall see how through Him demons are routed, oracles cease, and all magic and witchcraft is confounded.[42]

If we look back to 312 A.D., we can see a particular instance where the sign of the cross secured victory in battle. The Roman emperors Constantine I and Maxentius were in conflict with each other, and

---

[41] Quoted in Patti Maguire Armstrong, "4 Exorcists on Holy Hacks for Spiritual Protection," *Catholic News and Inspiration*, November 23, 2019, https://pattimaguirearmstrong.com/4-exorcists-on-holy-hacks-for-spiritual/. Fr. Gabriele Amorth, *An Exorcist Explains the Demonic: The Antics of Satan and His Army of Fallen Angels* (Manchester, NH: Sophia Institute Press, 2016), 123.

[42] St. Athanasius, *On the Incarnation*, no. 48, in *Christian Classics Ethereal Library*, https://www.ccel.org/ccel/athanasius/incarnation/incarnation.ix.html.

their forces were set to meet on the Milvian Bridge; Constantine was trying to bring his troops into the city of Rome, and Maxentius had his troops defending the bridge against Constantine's men. Now, Constantine and his men were vastly outnumbered, but he had a vision before the opposing forces met in battle. In the sky, he saw a cross, and underneath the cross were the words *in hoc signo vinces*, which means "by this sign, you will conquer." In this vision, God was promising Constantine victory in the battle if his soldiers painted the sign of the cross on their shields. And that is exactly what happened. That day, he had the words "do not be afraid," burned into his heart — and he won the Battle of the Milvian Bridge, and he became the sole ruler of the Roman Empire. Maxentius, on the other hand, drowned in the Tiber during the battle. This day marked the beginning of Constantine's conversion to Christianity, and it was through his conversion that Christianity was able to spread more freely throughout the civilized world.

It is not just in actual physical battles of human wars, such as the one at the Milvian Bridge, that Jesus' Cross can win victories. The Cross of Christ makes demons flee, and it makes Hell tremble. Lift high the Cross, and the Lord our God shall reign! It is so powerful that during a deliverance session with a victim afflicted with demons, the priest who is working to exorcise the demons or free the victim from interference will pray imperatively that the demon leave the victim and "go to the foot of the Cross." The "foot of the Cross" in deliverance ministry refers to the spiritual place of our redemption, a place that stands outside of time and space, for Calvary is the place where Satan was vanquished. For believers, the foot of the Cross is that spiritual place where all humans may spiritually retreat to receive refreshment and grace. It is the ultimate tribunal where Christ judges all demons, because it was where Satan himself was judged. Calvary is where God performed Judo on the enemy;[43] it is the place where the enemy's own power was used to defeat him. It is the place where God turned Satan's plans against him and used them to save the world.

## SACRED SCRIPTURE

The reading of Scripture is also an invaluable defense against the devil and his demons. St. John Chrysostom says that reading Scripture is not only necessary for the spiritual life but is also a particularly strong defense against demons:

> I desire that from those books you convey the letters and sense into your understanding, that so it may be purified when it receives the meaning of the writing. For if the devil will not dare to approach a house where a Gospel is lying, much less will any evil spirit, or any sinful nature, ever touch or enter a soul which bears about with it such sentiments as it contains. Sanctify then your soul, sanctify your body, by having these ever in your heart, and on your tongue. For if foul speech defiles and invites devils, it is clear that spiritual reading sanctifies and draws down the grace of the Spirit.[44]

St. Catherine of Bologna was an abbess of Augustinian nuns who lived in the 1400s. While she lived in communal poverty, pursued devout prayer, and had an unquenchable thirst for God, she suffered demonic assaults for five years, which led her to the brink of despair. At the end of her trials, however, she received a consoling vision that

---

[43]  Judo is an eastern form of martial arts self-defense in which you let your opponent rush you — with the goal of throwing your opponent by using his own weight against him.

[44]  St. John Chrysostom, "Homily 32 on the Gospel of John," in *Nicene and Post-Nicene Fathers*, first series, vol. 14, trans. Charles Marriott, ed. Philip Schaff (Buffalo, NY: Christian Literature Publishing, 1889), no. 3.

confirmed Christ's real presence in the Eucharist, and, through her trial, she grew spiritually. For the benefit of all of us in the Church Militant, she also composed *The Seven Spiritual Weapons*, which is a treatise on prayer and temptation. While all of her book is worth reading, I want to emphasize her seventh point, in which she agrees with St. John Chrysostom on the necessity of Scripture:

> The seventh weapon with which we can conquer our enemies is the memory of Holy Scripture which we must carry in our hearts and from which, as from a most devoted mother, we must take counsel in the things we have to do. Thus we read of the most prudent and consecrated virgin St. Cecilia where it says, "She always bore the gospel of Christ hidden in her heart." And with this weapon, our Savior Christ Jesus conquered and confounded the devil in the desert saying: "It is written," (Luke 4:1–13). Therefore, dearest sisters, let not the daily readings that you read in the choir and at table go without effect; and let the thoughts which you hear each day in the Gospels and epistles at Mass be new letters sent to you by your heavenly spouse. And with great and fervent love put them in your breast, and when you have more time, think about them; do this especially when you are in your cell so that you can better and more securely embrace gently and chastely the things which they command you. By doing this you will find yourselves continuously consoled because you will often receive news from the one whom you love above all else. O how sweet and gentle is the divine discourse of Christ Jesus in the soul of her who is truly enflamed by love of Him! Is not the Word Christ's own sweet and mellifluous mouth the evangelical doctrine? Certainly it is, and so how attentively you should listen to it and taste it. And here I put an end to the aforesaid weapons. But in this regard I beg you, dear

sisters, that you learn to use them wisely and never be found without them so that you can better obtain the triumph of victory against your adversaries.[45]

For one last thought on this immense power of God's spoken Word, let's look at a story from the life of St. Anthony of Padua, a famous preacher who lived in the 1200s and who particularly labored against heresy. One day, after he was expelled from a city full of heretics, St. Anthony walked to the nearby sea and started preaching to the fish: "You fish of the river and sea, listen to the word of God, because the heretics do not wish to hear it." A multitude of fish poked their heads out of the water and obediently listened to St. Anthony until he finished his sermon and dismissed them. The heretical inhabitants of the city, who had witnessed this miracle, were moved to repentance and reconciled with the Church.[46]

We see, then, that it is through the Rosary, general recourse to Mary, the use of the sign of the cross, speaking the Name of Jesus, and imprinting Scripture on our hearts that we are most effective in our day-to-day battles with demons. These are the tools that are given to all of us, and we all must use them if we want to be effective and capable in the battle for our souls and for the souls of those in the world around us.

For our priests, however, specifically those exorcists who are engaged in and responsible for combating the extraordinary activities of the devils, the prayers of the rites of exorcism are another a special weapon. Fr. Jeffrey Grob, an exorcist who studied the history of exorcism in detail for his doctoral dissertation, writes:

---

[45]  St. Catherine of Bologna, *The Seven Spiritual Weapons*, trans. Hugh Feiss and Daniela Re (Eugene, OR: Wipf and Stock, 2011), 41–42.

[46]  Fr. Sebastian White, O.P., "Saint Who," in *Magnificat* 25, no. 10 (December 2023), 335.

St. Cyprian (d. 258), bishop of Carthage, brings a different dimension to the discussion of the demonic. Drawing on his own experience as well as on the writings of Tertullian and Marcus Minucius Felix [one of the earliest Christian apologists to write in Latin (died ca. 250 A.D.)], Cyprian suggests that the actual words of exorcism inflict pain and torment on the demons. While St. Cyprian's hypothesis may not have had any direct bearing on the development of the ritual of exorcism in particular, it certainly reinforced the general importance of language and its usage in ritual action.... After the exorcism, the exorcist should ask the energumen what he/she experienced in his/her body and soul during the ritual. Words that apparently torment the devil should be used with greater stress and frequency.[47]

In short, exorcism is taking a demon, making him a POW, and torturing him. An exorcist does not follow the rules of the Geneva Convention when it comes to exorcism.

Quick notes: remember, we serve the Blessed Virgin Mary, and she is a twelve-star general. Pray the Holy Rosary and read the Holy Bible every day. In doing so, you will wound, inflict pain on, torment, and drive demons away from you and your family. Let's unite our prayers to the heel of Our Blessed Mother (see Gen. 3:15, Douay-Rheims). Let's unite our prayers to the Sword of St. Michael. And in this double unity, we will continue to deliver powerful blows to the kingdom of darkness, tearing down the gates of Hell.

---

[47] Jeffrey S. Grob, *A Major Revision of the Discipline on Exorcism: A Comparative Study of the Liturgical Laws in the 1614 and 1998 Rites of Exorcism* (Ph.D. diss., St. Paul University, Ottawa, 2006), 51, 99.

# Chapter 7

# Cristeros in the Culture War

In the 1920s, there was a civil war in Mexico. Radical secularists had taken over the government and, through fear and persecution, were trying to stamp out all practice of the Catholic Faith and the culture that supported it. In response to this anti-Catholic regime, faithful Mexicans formed a rebel group and called themselves the Cristeros — Soldiers of Christ. In the face of danger and death, atheism and persecution, the Cristeros fought for Christ. There were many martyrs in Mexico during this time, including Bl. Miguel Pro, a Jesuit priest who was executed by a firing squad for practicing his faith and for serving other Catholics in secret. When Bl. Miguel Pro stood before the firing squad, he had his arms outstretched in the form of a cross, and, just before he was shot, he shouted, *"Viva Cristo Rey!* — Long live Christ the King!" Like so many of the Cristeros, he lived and died for Christ.

Today, I believe that we have entered into a new era where we need Cristeros — but this time, here in the United States. We are at the edge of a cliff. We are at a tipping point. In a new way during the Obama administration, the culture of death gained serious ground through anti-life, anti-family policy changes; we saw this in the legalization of same-sex "marriage" in the Supreme Court case Obergefell v. Hodges and also in the Affordable Care Act, which, among other things, forced private companies to cover artificial birth control. Now our culture is continually pushing and testing the resolve and commitment of all Christians, especially Catholics. And the godless agenda of our culture of death has implications throughout the world because, for better or for worse, what happens in America affects the rest of the world.

How are we seeing the culture of death played out in our country? Look at what has happened or been encouraged during the Biden and Harris administration: tyrannical medical mandates; the increased persecution of pro-lifers; the efforts to remove parental guidance over children; the increased removal of Judeo-Christian symbols from public view; the legalization of recreational marijuana; "gay pride" gone wild; and countless other problems that all stem from the culture of death, issues that are attempts to undermine the very foundation of Christianity. All of these issues stem from the pits of Hell. Every single one of them is based on the ideology of moral relativism, which says that there is no absolute right or wrong and that everyone "makes his own truth." Clearly, this idea is nothing less than a diabolical attack on truth itself.

But even with the obvious onslaught against life, marriage, and religious liberty, there are still many Christians who remain ignorant, silent, or even complicit in these diabolical attacks against the Church. Understand this: if we remain silent in the face of these attacks against our faith, we are assisting the enemy. As Pope Leo XIII wrote: "To recoil before an enemy, or to keep silence when from all sides such clamors are raised against truth, is the part of a man either devoid of character or who entertains doubt as to the truth of what he professes to believe. In both cases such mode of behaving is base and is insulting to God, and both are incompatible with the salvation of mankind."[48]

---

[48]  Pope Leo XIII, encyclical letter *Sapientiae Christianae* (January 10, 1890), no. 14.

What can we do, then? Well, I'll tell you what I have done. I have dedicated my life to promoting the culture of life in the face of the culture of death, to promoting everything that is good, true, and beautiful. We must be prepared to continue fighting the good fight of faith — these days we're living in demand it of us. We must not be silent; we must speak the truth in charity for the dignity of human life, for traditional biblical marriage, and for religious liberty. In this third millennium, we must be even more committed to being Cristeros. We need to stay informed about what the culture of death is doing, and we need to live in a state of grace. There are so many people today who have no sense of moral clarity; the generations to come are counting on our resolve to stand up for Jesus and to lift high the Cross: *Viva Cristo Rey!*

In ancient times, master swordsmiths perfected the art of forging the ideal blade for battle. They knew how to combine the right ingredients to create a metal that was strong enough to hold an edge but flexible enough so as not to break in the midst of a fight. The different elements were brought together in fire, melted down, and then blended together. Again, in fire, the metal was heated up, allowing the swordsmith to fold it upon itself. It would then be hammered flat, and, through the pressure of the pounding, the folded layers would adhere to each other. This process would be repeated dozens of times, thereby creating dozens and dozens of layers in the blade. The end result would be a weapon strong enough to keep that sharp edge and flexible enough not to break.

This is exactly what we, as soldiers of Christ, are meant to be. God is always trying to forge us, sometimes under very intense conditions, in order to build us into strong, disciplined, spiritual warriors. A warrior has the ability to stand up at a moment's notice and courageously defend what is honorable — and to do so with deep conviction. He is, at the same time, able to master his passions and to lead with a strong, gentle spirit. We can always look to St. Joseph for a model of this warrior spirit, especially in the face of demonic warfare. St. Joseph, most valiant, terror of demons, pray for us! He will help us to stay battle ready and to know that the Spirit of God is the master swordsmith that forges us all into fighting shape.

In the end, we have the certainty that truth will triumph over lies, light over darkness, and good over evil. So stand firm, Catholics, and rush to the battle lines with Jesus in your heart, a rosary in one hand, and a Bible in the other. No matter what happens, no matter how each particular battle turns out, we know that Christ the King wins the war. *Viva Cristo Rey!* He is our hope! Jesus Christ came to save the lost, the last, and the least, and Jesus Christ heals, Jesus Christ saves, and Jesus Christ sets us free.

# CHAPTER 8

# Observing the Battlefield:
# Tactics for Success

CONFUSION, WHICH IS THE smoke of Satan, is enveloping the battlefield. In order to defeat the forces of chaos, we need purity of doctrine, clarity of words, firmness of example, and an accordance of soul and of works, for St. Paul teaches: "And if the bugle gives an indistinct sound, who will get ready for battle?" (1 Cor. 14:8).

There are many different reasons why more Catholic Christians don't stand up and fight for the truth. Distraction, insecurity, selfishness, or being tied down by some habitual sin could all be part of it. But another reason some won't or don't stand in the gap and fight is ignorance. Many of our brothers and sisters are what you might call "low-information Catholics." Many people find that keeping themselves in the dark about the intentions and attacks of those who want to destroy what is of God, keeping themselves in "blissful ignorance," is an easier way to get through life. Choosing to remain ignorant is an age-old problem. We all have some version of a little voice in our head that, if we let it, will convince us that things aren't really that bad — even though in reality they are falling apart. The truth is, the more we know about those who are trying to destroy what is holy and noble, the more we understand their tactics, the better chance we have of engaging successfully in the fight with them.

As we face off with these real evils and the people who carry them, we do also need to remember that we should never violate God's law in the process of knowing the enemy. I realize that it can be difficult to hear about the different attacks and battles that are going on in our world. It can feel like too much at times to see the churches that are vandalized, the priests that are attacked, and the good people who are persecuted in their businesses for speaking the truth. To combat the instinct to return violence with violence, it is imperative that we study and remember the Word of God: "Have I not commanded you? Be strong and of good courage; be not frightened, neither be dismayed; for the Lord your God is with you wherever you go" (Josh. 1:9). We must be ready for the battle, ready to meet it morally and ethically, because whether we ignore it or not, the fight is upon us. Each of us must consider our role in the fight and then decide to act on a higher level of commitment and involvement in the battle. And we need to call others to arms as well. How do we do this? At this point in this book, it should not surprise you that, before everything else, you need to sit down and pray. Remember the words of St. Josemaría Escrivá: "First, prayer; then, atonement; in the third place … action."[49]

So, you know that the first step to being prepared for the battle, and to keeping on with the good fight when you're in the middle of it, is to start with prayer. What comes next? Here's a checklist for you, to keep you on the right track.

✠ Increase your prayer and fasting a little at a time.

---

[49] St. Josemaría Escrivá, *The Way*, no. 82; available at "Prayer," *Escriva.org*, https://escriva.org/en/camino/prayer/.

☩ Stay close to God through frequent reception of the sacraments.

☩ Increase your Scripture reading.

☩ Be vocal in defending and spreading the truth, according to your state and position in life.

☩ Don't make excuses for not doing the above things.

If you need some extra motivation, first remember that it is impossible for us to realize just how much our families are counting on us. Then, think about all the souls that you come into contact with every day. Next, think about the lives to come that you have never met and never will meet in this life. Fight for them all! Souls are at stake! We need to toughen up, be ready for this battle, and stick it out once we find ourselves in the middle of it! There's too much at stake — too many souls at stake — to be lazy and soft on this battlefield. As Archbishop Fulton Sheen said, "To be worthy of the name Christian … we, too, must thirst for the spread of the divine love; and if we do not thirst, then we shall never be invited to sit down at the banquet of life."[50] Christ demands zeal!

There is nothing anywhere in the Gospels that even remotely implies that Jesus is okay with us being lukewarm or mediocre with living our faith. In fact, it's pretty clear that the exact opposite is the case. Look at these verses, which are just a few of their sort that come directly from our Lord. Scripture is full of many more:

☩ "I came to cast fire upon the earth; and would that it were already kindled!" (Luke 12:49).

---

[50] Venerable Archbishop Fulton J. Sheen, from *The Cries of Jesus from the Cross: An Anthology* (Manchester, NH: Sophia Institute Press, 2018), 239–40.

✣ "Because you are lukewarm, and neither cold nor hot, I will spew you out of my mouth" (Rev. 3:16).

✣ "And he answered, 'You shall love the Lord your God with all your heart, and with all your soul, and with all your strength, and with all your mind, and your neighbor as yourself'" (Luke 10:27).

We each have free will. We each have the ability to make the choice whether or not we are going to let the ways of this world water us down. It can be easy to allow the concerns of this life to throw water on the fire that Christ wishes were already ignited in our souls. It is very easy to allow ourselves to give into the temptation of being lazy when it comes to keeping ourselves sharp.

Look back at that checklist of five tactics for success on the spiritual battlefield, and ask yourself: Do you have a daily prayer life? How often are you getting to the sacrament of Confession? Are you taking time to read Scripture — often? Are you maintaining the temple of the Holy Spirit — that is, your body — with some exercise and decent eating habits? As a soldier of Christ, you have the duty to keep yourself sharp in body, mind, and soul. If you have been given the care of other people, then you have the duty to be sharp for them as well. You cannot lead them to the glory of Heaven if you have little or no understanding of what that means. Without the grace of God, it is impossible to fulfill our duty. So go to the Source. Cooperate with the grace of God. Do what you were put here to do! Get ready for the battle, because Christ demands zeal, and others are counting on that zeal from you.

I've got one word for you: hero! Most of us, at one time or another, dream of being the hero. We see ourselves flying into some intense situation in some dramatic way, where we outsmart or beat up the bad guy, then disable a bomb with three seconds left on the timer, right before it blows up half the hemisphere. A lot of us live the hero dream out through the movies, some of us through novels, and some of us in sports and cyberspace. Maybe we watch Captain America kick the villains all over the place in the latest Marvel movie and, once again, save the world. Maybe, as we read and watch *Lord of the Rings*, we cheer for Eowyn as she destroys the prince of darkness, revealing her golden hair as she cuts him down with her triumphant cry: "I am no man!" Maybe we like to step into cyberspace or the world of gaming to conquer, crush, and dominate the bad guys — and then, of course, we save the world.

For some of us, these hero dreams happened when we were kids. But as we get older, too often we see ourselves as having moved past that so-called childish phase. Maybe this is you. Maybe you've become so sophisticated or intellectual and mature that the idea of saving the world just doesn't flip your trigger. Or maybe you're so distracted or anxious about life in general that the hero dream has been buried under a pile of worry or insecurity, and you're not able to see it clearly.

The truth is, because you are a child of God, you were made to be a hero. God cut you from hero cloth. You were created not just to entertain yourself with hero movies and games but to learn from them and then to actually go live by them and *be* the hero! You or I might never beat up a bad guy and then disable that bomb seconds before it's about to annihilate the world, but no matter your state in life, you are the hero of the lives that God has given to you to care for. You are the hero of their worlds. Those people in your care see you, and they watch how you take on the attacks of the world, the flesh, and the devil. They watch how you deal with your own weaknesses and what you do to rise above your failings to defeat the bad guys — especially the ones within your own heart.

So go to the source of heroic strength daily: Jesus in His Word and sacraments. He will get you ready for battle, because heroes need to stay sharp and alert. Souls are counting on you. Trust God, pray the Rosary, and remember that this is actually a great time to be a Catholic Christian, because we know that we are on the winning side. God is not dead. Nietzsche is dead, and God is not even tired.

One last word: we should pray with strength, not out of fear. Demons can tell when we pray with fear and doubt. Remember what I told you earlier, that in one of Jesus' revelations to St. Faustina, he said, "Fight like a knight, so that I can reward you. Do not be unduly fearful, because you are not alone."[51] Our prayers should have the strength and character of rich, confidant voices. And because prayer has an offensive nature to it, a group of us praying together should sound like drums being pounded by an overlord or taskmaster, with a hundred men pulling the oars in unison at ramming speed. Picture a Roman soldier about to go into battle. As he stands in formation, rhythmically pounding on his shield, in sync with his fellow soldiers, they all together, slowly, methodically, and with quiet intensity, strike fear into the heart of their enemies. This is exactly how we Catholics should look when we are joined together in prayer.

---

[51] St. Maria Faustina Kowalska, *Diary*, no. 1760.

# Part II

## Soldiers in Spiritual Warfare: Prayer in Action

IN THE FIRST PART of this book, I wanted to tell you what prayer is all about, why it's important, the meaning behind it, and how it helps us go on the offensive with the devil. In this next section of the book, I'm going to share a number of particular encounters with you, some episodes either from my life or from the lives of some of my friends and family, where we could see prayer and grace taking on the power of Hell — and dominating it. My prayer for you here is that, in reading these stories, you will begin to recognize the similar moments in your own life for what they really are: moments where prayer is your own offensive weapon against the gates of Hell.

# CHAPTER 1

# No Chance Encounters

IN 1999, I WAS invited to speak at the South Texas Men's Conference, sponsored by the Archdiocese of San Antonio, Texas. It was held right before the 2000 Jubilee Year, and the excitement and anticipation both for the event itself and for the coming year was tangible in the crowd of the five thousand men gathered together at the convention center. There was an impressive list of speakers at this conference: Scott Hahn, Marcus Grodi, Jeff Cavins, Curtis Martin — men of God and men of valor who have touched my life in profound ways with their teachings and their love for Scripture. I was honored to be on the same platform.

As the conference finished early that Saturday evening, and I left for the airport and boarded the plane for the three-hour flight back to California, I began thinking about getting home, tackling my boys, hugging my daughter, and spending a quiet evening in my wife's arms. There weren't many people on that plane, probably only fifteen of us, and about eighty-five empty seats, so the flight attendant told us we could sit anywhere we wanted. I made a beeline for the very back of the plane, where I could see that I'd have four seats to myself, with no one else around me for ten rows. I was tired from the conference, and I was looking forward to stretching out across those four seats as soon as the seatbelt sign went off. I took out a copy of *This Rock* magazine, thinking I could catch up on some spiritual reading.

As I began reading, I suddenly sensed danger and the presence of evil, probably thanks to my police training and also the gift of discernment. When I looked up, I saw a woman walking down the aisle toward me. She was really exaggerating her walk, moving her hips from left to right as if she were walking the runway at a beauty pageant. I noticed that she was dressed very immodestly. As she walked, her long hair bounced from left to right, and she ran her fingers through it several times. She was pretty, and she knew it.

She had the attention of every male on the plane, from the stewards to the passengers. I said to myself, *Okay, time to take custody of the eyes,* and I looked down and began reading my magazine again. Well, lo and behold, this woman walked all the way to the back of the plane, passing all those empty seats, and sat right next to me. The flight attendant told us to fasten our seatbelts, and we took off.

My police training had me thinking that this lady was a prostitute. I didn't want to make it obvious that I didn't want to sit next to her, but I decided that when we were able to unbuckle our seatbelts, I would simply find another seat on the plane. For any man (Catholic or not), sitting next to a young, scantily clad prostitute whose perfume could be detected ten rows away is a near occasion of sin, unwise and imprudent. It was especially true for someone like me, happily married as I am. So, I looked out the window, and I focused on reading my magazine.

At least, I tried to. But she kept trying to talk to me as she applied fire-red lipstick and brushed her long hair. I exchanged some polite pleasantries with her, telling her that I had been in San Antonio on business and was headed back home. She replied that she was on business, too, and then she moved right in with some sexual innuendos. I was caught off guard at how bold and brazen she was.

At first, I felt intimidated. I had dealt with women like this during my law enforcement days. Often, they were cold, calculating, calloused women who would steal anything that wasn't nailed down. But I also knew that they were wounded sinners; so many men had lied to them, beat them, humiliated them, cursed at them, stolen from them, and used them that they had developed hardened hearts. Their jaded outlooks were the consequence of a life of sin like that, but I also knew how strong the pull of lust, promiscuity, and fornication can be, and how it can enslave a person. The Gospel tells us this plainly: "Jesus answered them, 'Truly, truly, I say to you, everyone who commits sin is a slave to sin'" (John 8:34). And in St. Paul, we read: "Do you not know that if you yield yourselves to anyone as obedient slaves, you are slaves of the one whom you obey, either of sin, which leads to death, or of obedience, which leads to righteousness?" (Rom. 6:16).

She didn't stick to innuendoes for long; she quickly began speaking in plain seduction, invading my space and privacy. I tried to intimidate her by telling her that I was a Los Angeles deputy sheriff, but she was undeterred. She even responded immediately by saying in sensuous tones that she gave special discounts to law enforcement officers!

At this point I heard the words of Jesus in my mind: "You will know the truth, and the truth will make you free" (John 8:32). For some reason, I sensed that this woman was a fallen-away Catholic. I reached into my carry-on and took out the Holy Bible — my sword. She leaned over and tried to whisper in my ear the different things that she was offering and her price for each one. I said to myself in a soft whisper, "Speak to me, Lord; your servant is listening" (see 1 Sam. 3: 10). I opened my Bible, and it fell open to 2 Timothy 1:6–8: "Hence I remind you to rekindle the gift of God that is within you through the laying on of my hands; for God did not give us a spirit of timidity but a spirit of power and love and self-control. Do not be ashamed then of testifying to our Lord." I flipped to another page and read silently again, "Do not be afraid, but speak and do not be silent; for I am with you" (Acts 18:9–10). I turned to one last page, and my eyes fell upon "Little children, you are of God, and have overcome them; for he who is in you is greater than he who is in the world" (1 John 4:4).

I felt like Popeye when he's just opened a can of spinach! Now I was ready to speak aloud, ready like a lion who could breathe fire — if such a thing were possible. I turned to her quickly and, with a surge of inspiration, I said, "Shame on you! Don't you know that you are already married to someone? I know that you are a fallen-away Catholic, and you belong to *Jesus*. You are his bride — you are consecrated to him!"

She looked at me, stunned, and admitted that she was a Catholic who had not been inside a Catholic Church since she made her first Holy Communion at the age of seven. She also shared that she had been a prostitute since she was eighteen. She was now twenty-eight, living in Las Vegas, where she plied her trade. I also suspected that she was a drug addict who sold her body to support her habit.

So, I had two options:

1.  I could get up, move to a different seat, and go back to reading my magazine, telling myself, *Tough luck — she's all screwed up; she doesn't know Jesus. She's on her way to Hell.*

2.  I could listen to Jesus' words: "Go into all the world and preach the gospel to the whole creation.... In my name they will cast out demons" (Mark 16:15, 17). As the *Catechism* states, "The true apostle is on the lookout for occasions of announcing Christ by word, either to unbelievers ... or to the faithful."[52]

---

[52]  Decree on the Apostolate of the Laity *Apostolicam Actuositatem* (November 18, 1965), no. 6; quoted in CCC 905.

I knew this was not a chance encounter but had been ordained by God. How did I know this? Again, as the *Catechism* says, "Divine providence works also through the actions of creatures. To human beings God grants the ability to cooperate freely with his plans" (CCC 323). So I began to tell her about salvation history and how God has provided His Son Jesus Christ to save, sanctify, and set her free. Her countenance began to change from one of sexual aggression to humility, and, suddenly, I could tell that the gospel was making sense to her. I knew that her heart longed for God (see Ps. 42:1). As I spoke to her about the Lord Jesus, she covered her chest with her arms. I took off my jacket and lent it to her so she would not feel embarrassed. She said, "That's funny, I've never been embarrassed to expose myself before any man, but I feel embarrassed in front of you."

Since we had a three-hour flight ahead of us, I began sharing the beauty of our Catholic Faith with this lost soul. I told her that many people will miss Heaven by twelve inches — the distance from their head to their heart. I showed her John 3:16 — "For God [the greatest lover] so loved the world [the greatest amount of people] that he gave his only Son [the greatest gift], that whoever believes in him should not perish [the greatest hope] but have eternal life [the greatest reward]" — and I told her how this is the greatest love story ever told because it involves every single one of us and God.

She began to weep. Three hours on an airplane began to heal so many years of having a heart broken by sin. She asked me if God could ever forgive her for the past ten years of her life as a prostitute and all that came with it. I shared the following verses with her:

- ✢ "Though your sins are like scarlet, they shall be as white as snow" (Isa. 1:18).

- ✢ "The Lord is merciful and gracious, slow to anger and abounding in steadfast love" (Ps. 103:8).

✠ "I, I am He who blots out your transgressions for my own sake, and I will not remember your sins" (Isa. 43:25).

As she cried tears of pain, healing, and joy, I shared Joel 2:25 with her: "I will restore to you the years which the swarming locust has eaten."

As the plane began its descent into Burbank, she said to me, "Every time you show me something from the Bible, my heart starts burning — and I know it's true." She used the same words that the disciples on the road to Emmaus had used about the risen Lord Jesus Christ after He had vanished from their sight (see Luke 24:32). When we landed, we walked together toward the baggage claim area. I let her keep my jacket so that she would not bring undue attention to herself. I had a Catholic prayer book and a booklet called "Let There Be Light" in my carry-on, and I gave these to her as we were waiting for our luggage. She said tearfully, "I want to have Jesus in my heart." So I said to her, "Let's pray," and she asked, "Where?" "Right here!"

She closed her eyes, and I led her into a heartfelt prayer of repentance and willingness to open her heart to Jesus and proclaim Him as her Lord and Savior. Weeping, she repeated every single word I said. I told her to go to a Catholic Church as soon as possible and make an appointment with a priest to go to confession.

Her parting words to me were, "I had bad intentions when I saw you in the back of that plane. I thought you were some wealthy businessman — and I know my way around wealthy businessmen. I've been with over one thousand men in the last ten years, and in that time, they have lied to me, raped me, abused me, hit me, stolen from me, cursed at me, disrespected me, you name it. But you are the first man in my life to talk to me about Jesus."

I responded, "Whatever good I do comes from God, and I thank Him for it." We said good-bye, and I wished her God's blessing. I hope she followed through with her newfound commitment; if she did, I will see her again — this time in her white baptismal garments, when Jesus comes back at the resurrection of the elect.

As people of faith, we have an advantage in life. We wake up with a purpose. We have a sense of mission, and we know our lives have enduring meaning. People who are in situations like this prostitute was in when she first approached me are "wandering generalities" who serve the unholy trinity of "me, myself, and I" as a result of their sinful lifestyles. But we serve a God of resurrection. We can share with confidence the Word of God, no matter what circumstances we find ourselves in. There are no chance encounters!

Chapter 2

# My Wife Prayed for Me

Genesis 2:18 tells us: "Then the Lord God said, 'It is not good that the man should be alone; I will make him a helper fit for him.'" The Hebrew word for *helper* here is *ezer*, which means someone who aids, protects, and defends, especially in battle. Peter Lombard, a scholastic theologian and Catholic bishop who lived in the twelfth century, reiterated that the role of Eve and of all women is therefore to be "helpers" for their husbands in the battle of life — warriors who help save the souls of their husbands and children. As Lombard reminds us, "Eve was not taken from the feet of Adam to be his slave, nor from his head to be his lord, but from his side to be his partner."[53]

If you want to know what that looks like in the real world, here's a story for you. In June of 2016, I was admitted to Mercy Gilbert Medical Center for shortness of breath. I had been doing yard work, and my wife noticed that I had labored breathing. Her nursing sensibilities kicked in, and she insisted I go to the hospital. She took me herself, and she would not take no for an answer. Once we were in the ER, the doctors diagnosed me with a saddle pulmonary embolism and sent me right to the intensive care unit. It was a

---

[53] Peter Lombard, *Sentences* 1:2:18, quoted in William E. Phipps, *Genesis and Gender: Biblical Myths of Sexuality and Their Cultural Impact* (New York: Praeger, 1989), 107.

77

life-threatening condition that meant I had a large blood clot lodged right where my pulmonary artery divides in two, right where it is supposed to supply blood to both lungs — and that mean that blood flow to both lungs was being obstructed. The doctor told my wife and me that because of the size of the blockage — 90 percent — they were surprised I was even able to breathe. And then he told us that if we had waited one more day to come in, I wouldn't have survived. I even overheard one doctor say to another, "I'm surprised he's still alive." They told me later that they have a special name for a blockage like that: a widow-maker.

The whole time that I was in the hospital, I was running through prayers in my head: I was praying the Act of Contrition, the Jesus Prayer, the Rosary, and the Chaplet of Divine Mercy, and I was talking to the Lord as one talks to a friend. I was at peace. I told my wife that I was ready to meet the Lord (Rom. 14:8, NABRE: "For if we live, we live for the Lord, and if we die, we die for the Lord; so then, whether we live or die, we are the Lord's"). I was actually joyful that I was about to go to my exit interview in front of the tribunal of Christ my King. I had gone to confession a few days before, and I knew that I was in a state of grace. When I was in my hospital room, with all kinds of IVs and attachments to my body, and the doctors had left, I looked into my wife's eyes, and I could see that she looked sad.

But then, like the lioness that she is, she said, "I still need you, the kids still need you, your grandkids still need you." I could almost read her mind, and it was like she was saying, "You ain't going anywhere, not yet." She began reciting vocal prayers of healing and supplication to God, and she was crying at the same time for God to save me from death: "In the days when he was in the flesh, he offered prayers and supplications with loud cries and tears to the one who was able to save him from death, and he was heard because of his reverence" (Heb. 5:7, NABRE). With much reverence, *she put her hand on my heart as she prayed for three hours, non-stop,* and I finally fell asleep at total peace, knowing that the two persons that loved me the most were in the room with me: my God and my wife. The doctors thought I was not going to make it through the night — but I woke up the next morning.

When the doctor examined me again, he didn't know what had happened. He was completely bewildered as he looked at my new X-rays and CAT scans, and he said, "What happened to you overnight was a miracle. Ninety percent of the saddle pulmonary embolism is gone." But I knew what had happened: Anita had prayed for me in the hospital for those three hours, with her right hand on my heart. She had prayed and cried, and prayed and cried, and I was healed the next day — when both doctors had said it was medically impossible to be healed that fast. They said there was no drug that could dissolve a 90 percent blockage from a saddle pulmonary embolism in eight hours. According to all the rules of medicine, I should be dead right now, but I am alive and preaching the Catholic Gospel because I have a believing wife who is a prayer warrior: "For the unbelieving husband is consecrated through his wife, and the unbelieving wife is consecrated through her husband.… Wife, how do you know whether you will save your husband?" (1 Cor. 7:14, 16).

I know of at least six reasons why my wife's prayers for me were effective and answered by God, and they are all from Scripture. Likely there are more, but for now, husbands and wives, learn from this list, and take care of each other. Pray for each other. Your prayers can help each other in a way no other prayers can.

1. My wife has authority over my body (1 Cor. 7:4). Does a wife have *spiritual* authority over her husband? No, but she has rights over his body.

2. My wife was in a state of grace when she prayed for me that night (James 5:16).

3. She prayed sincerely, with tears streaming down her face (Heb. 5:7; 2 Kings 20:5).

4. Her prayer was very specific (Matt. 7:7).

5. Her prayer was according to God's will for me (Matt. 6:10).

6. She did not put her hand on my head, because she is not the head of household; she put her hand on my heart, because, as Pope Pius XI taught, "For if the man is the head, the woman is the heart, and as he occupies the chief place in ruling, so she may and ought to claim for herself the chief place in love."[54] On this last point, something to consider: some biblical scholars say that when Eve was formed out of Adam's rib, that rib was the one that covered and protected his heart.

[54] Pope Pius XI, *Casti Connubii* (December 31, 1930), no. 27.

# Chapter 3

# Light and Dark: The Chaplet of St. Michael the Archangel

*"But if we walk in the light, as he is in the light, we have fellowship with one another, and the blood of Jesus his Son cleanses us from all sin. If we say we have no sin, we deceive ourselves, and the truth is not in us. If we confess our sins, he is faithful and just, and will forgive our sins and cleanse us from all unrighteousness."*

1 John 1:7–9

In the summer of 2020, Anita and I flew to Denver to participate in a small conference that was given by noted exorcist Fr. Chad Ripperger and by Kyle Clement, his case facilitator. The conference was at the Renaissance Denver Stapleton Hotel. You probably noticed already that it was during the time of the government-imposed lockdowns that came in response to the  Covid-19 virus.

We arrived at our hotel, checked into our rooms, and recessed for the evening, resting in anticipation of the conference that would start the next morning. But when we woke up, the lights were out in the hotel, and in fact all of the electricity was out. We had already planned on most of the attendees not being able to be there in person because of the lockdowns, and we had set things up for them to join us virtually in an online conference setting. But now the recording equipment, the laptops, the microphones — everything was off, and we were scheduled to start in thirty minutes. There were about twenty of us there on site, including the speakers and the equipment operators, and we were all just sort of looking at each other, dumbfounded, not knowing what to do next.

But then Fr. Ripperger said something to Dr. Dan Schneider (a retired soldier and a theologian from Franciscan University of Steubenville), and Dan snapped to attention in his old soldier-like way and said to the group, "Let's pray the St. Michael the Archangel Chaplet." We gathered around Dan, and he began leading us in this beautiful chaplet. I had vaguely heard about this prayer a short while before from Dan himself and from Kyle Clement. Like Kyle, Dan is also a lay member of Fr. Ripperger's exorcism team. We were praying in darkness as Dan led the prayers, and then, within seconds of Dan finishing the chaplet, all of the lights and the electricity came back on. Right on schedule, we proceeded with the Spiritual Warfare conference, which was miraculously available to all of the virtual attendees. As I saw the lights go on, I knew it was not a coincidence; it was, very clearly, an act of God. "And God said, 'Let there be light'; and there was light" (Gen. 1:3).

The Chaplet of St. Michael the Archangel is also sometimes called the Rosary of the Angels. It was given by St. Michael himself to a Portuguese Carmelite nun, Sr. Antónia de Astónaco, in a private revelation, and it was approved by Pope Pius IX in 1851. St. Michael promised that anyone who made a habit of praying this chaplet would be accompanied by an angel from each of the nine choirs of angels during each reception of Holy Communion. He also promised that he and all of the angels would always assist those who pray this chaplet, and that, after death, they would be delivered from

Purgatory. He also said that these benefits and blessings would be extended to their direct family members.[55] This prayer is therefore a powerful way to call upon St. Michael the Archangel and on all of the nine choirs of angels to engage in spiritual battle with you.[56]

Not surprisingly, since he was the one who led us in the Chaplet when the power had gone out, Dan Schneider wrote an email to me once about the reasons why this prayer is so powerful and how it helps us in spiritual warfare. Dan really gets the way that prayer is a weapon, and this one especially:

> During times when we struggle to find the words asking for God's help, we should work in the St. Michael Chaplet as needed, especially when we feel push back from the enemy and feel discouraged. The St. Michael Chaplet is very effective. It should be used as needed, i.e., when movement is needed quickly. In military language, this is like a claymore mine used to halt the enemy's infiltration — or like when soldiers retreat, they blow up the bridge with C4 after they have crossed it to prevent their enemies from attacking them. Since we don't know which choir of demons is attacking us, the chaplet invokes each choir of angels to militate directly to the situation. So, if we are up against a principality class demon that may be militating against our vocation, by invoking principalities as part of the chaplet, we often get some positive movement. And since are asking for obedience, charity, and humility, the angels bring that charism to the situation.

---

[55] National Centre for Padre Pio, "Devotion to St. Michael the Archangel," https://www.padrepio.org/pray/devotion-to-st-michael-the-archangel/.

[56] For direct guidance on how to pray the St. Michael Chaplet, see Cate Von Dohlen, "How to Pray the St. Michael Chaplet," *Hallow*, https://hallow.com/blog/how-to-pray-the-st-michael-chaplet/; it is also available in the appendix at the end of this book.

I picture Our Lady on a throne with her crown, the Queen of the Angels, as we pray. With her right hand, she signals the seraphim to fly to our assistance like fighter jets flying off a Navy aircraft carrier. As we pray to the angels in order, I see Our Lady with her right hand, commanding each choir of angels to fly to our assistance, just like the aircraft crew makes hand gestures and sends off fighter jets to do battle. This is what she does with all the choirs of angel as we pray each decade.

Remember, angels go where they are called and demons go where they are not resisted, so the Chaplet of St. Michael invites the nine choirs of angels in order and they bring their charism, which is antithetical to the demons of whatever class are operating against your son, daughter, your family, your marriage, or your situation. The Chaplet of St. Michael also invokes the three known archangels from Scripture; they engage and come to our assistance as well. The Chaplet also fosters a greater devotion to our guardian angels and keeps them active and present to the situation at hand. That is just what we saw happening that day at the hotel, when all the lights went out, and we called on St. Michael and all of our angels to come and help us.

That conference was not the only time I've seen Genesis 1:3 — "And God said, 'Let there be Light'; and there was light" — play out right before me. In January of 2024, I was invited to speak at St. Anthony of Padua Church in Hammonton, New Jersey. Anita and I were staying at a nearby hotel, and someone from the church came to pick us up before the talk. My talk was going to be about Catholic spiritual warfare, once in English and then, on the second evening, in Spanish. When we got there, we met Fr. David Rivera, a young, solid, orthodox pastor who was wearing his black cassock, something I always take as a good sign. He told me, "We've had a blackout since yesterday; there was a heavy storm with lots of rain, and we haven't had electricity in this area for almost twenty-four hours. The electrical company that services this area said they're not sure how much longer this section of the town will be blacked out." Fr. Rivera asked if I were okay giving the conference in a dark church, and of course I agreed to go ahead with it. It reminded me of the Saturday night Easter Vigil Liturgy, during which the deacon proclaims loudly as he and the priest process inside the dark Church: "The Light of Christ!"

Fr. Rivera, together with some nuns and parishioners, began lighting every candle they could find inside the church and brought out as many as they could find from the sanctuary and sacristy. They began placing them along the aisle on the floor all around the church in an attempt to bring in some light. People were coming into the church as it neared 7 p.m., which was the start time. I'm sure some people probably thought this was part of the conference — as if it would add something to the atmosphere to have the church dark as they walked into a spiritual warfare conference.

When it was time to start, Father walked up to the ambo, greeted the people, introduced me, and then began an opening prayer, which ended with the prayer to St. Michael the Archangel. At the same time, the nuns had gone into the side chapel, where Father had placed the Holy Eucharist in the monstrance for them for adoration. As soon as he finished his last prayer, Father walked out of the ambo and then signaled for me to walk up and proceed. As soon as I walked up and, by force of habit, adjusted the microphone to my height, all the lights suddenly turned on. We were all silent for a few seconds, and all I could say was, "Let there be light, and there was light!"

Like the time that Dan had led all of us in the St. Michael Chaplet together, this was another moment of grace in my life where God was reminding me that He is with us — He is with the Church. He has everything under control, and we can trust in Him no matter what. For all of us there that night, and for all of you reading this story now, it was another piece of evidence of the power of prayer.

# Chapter 4

# Prayer: Torment of Demons

My wife and I are parishioners of Our Lady of Guadalupe in Queen Creek, Arizona. There is a small but beautiful adoration chapel at the parish, and we adore the Lord there for one hour every Tuesday morning, starting at midnight. There is a security code to get into the chapel so our Lord is kept safe, though the code is available to any parishioner who wants it, meaning well-intentioned people can go inside anytime to make a visit.

One day, after our Wednesday Men's Gathering, I decided to spend some time with our Lord in adoration. There had been a lot of painful stories from my brothers in our group that night, and I wanted to take their petitions to our Lord in the adoration chapel. It was about 9 p.m., and I was in there by myself. But after about ten minutes of silent prayer, I saw another Hispanic gentleman come in, looking like he was in excruciating pain.

This man fell prostrate on the floor, face down, and, within less than a minute, he started having what looked like a grand mal seizure. It reminded me of some things I had seen when I was a cop on the streets of Los Angeles. He started speaking in a deep, guttural voice, but it wasn't in English or Spanish. I looked at him, stunned, and kept watching him as he shook on the ground and spoke in that undecipherable language. I kept on praying, but now my prayers were in supplication for this poor soul, as I was thinking that what looked like a grand mal seizure was actually a diabolic manifestation (unfortunately, I have seen both many times). Suddenly, he got up, startling me, and stared right at me for about three seconds, with his eyes jet black; then he ran out of the adoration chapel. I said to myself, "Oh no, this is not good."

I walked outside, following him and trying to keep an eye on him, and I found him bent over some bushes on the church patio — he was dry heaving, trying to vomit. I asked him "Sir, are you okay? Do you need me to call the paramedics?" He understood English, but he responded to me in Spanish. He told me his first name, Abel, and, not at all surprising to me, he told me that he was possessed. I asked him if he needed a ride home, or maybe a bottle of water? I was trying to calm him down in any way I could think of, as he was clearly beyond stressed out. But he didn't want a ride home or any water; he said he wanted company and someone to talk to. I told him that I was in no rush to get home, and I offered to listen to him.

He was from Mexico, he said, but he had come here to Arizona as an illegal immigrant. When he was still in Mexico, he was involved for many years in La Santa Muerte — a Satan-worshipping cult and effectively the religion of the cartels. He had been active in that cult for about eight years. During that time, he said, he'd consulted witches, played the Ouija board, and been involved in astral projection, which is when the soul travels out of the body in a demonic parody of saintly bilocation. He also told me that his roommates told him that, multiple times, when they went to wake him up for work in the morning, they had found him levitating over his bed while he slept.

When he told me that he was seeing a Catholic priest for treatment and shared that priest's name, I knew he was telling the truth: he had given me the name of the exorcist of the diocese of Phoenix. I went ahead and gave him a bottle of water, and I tried to calm him down, assuring him that he was on the road to being healed and liberated and advising him that he must follow the instructions of the exorcist exactly. He said that the priest had instructed him to pay visits to Our Lord in the Blessed Sacrament and to try to stay in silent prayer as long as he could, but that, for now, he could only be inside the adoration chapel for about a minute or two before he would be tormented by a diabolic manifestation.

As we were talking, he suddenly stopped and stared at me, and then he asked, "Are you Jesse Romero?" When I said I was, Abel asked me, "Please, please, can you pray for me? I need as many people as possible praying for me." I assured him that I would pray the Chaplet of Divine Mercy for him for the next nine days, that I would make a novena of it. He asked me, in a lot of distress, to actually pray for him, not to just say that I would to make him feel better. To reassure him that I would keep my promise, I told him I'd write his name in the notes on my phone as a reminder. He insisted that I take his number too, and he asked me to please text him after I was done praying for him. He wanted to have that extra reassurance that I would keep my promise to him. And I did promise that I would call him each day for the next nine days when I finished the Chaplet for him.

At that point, we said goodnight, and we both drove our separate ways. But the next day, at 3:00 p.m., I stopped what I was doing, and I asked my wife to join me in praying the Chaplet of Divine Mercy. Once we started praying, we finished in about six or seven minutes, and then suddenly my phone rang, and it was that man. He was hyperventilating, like he had just run a 10K. He asked me, "Did you just finish praying for me?" When I said yes, he told me, "The demons inside me said, 'Tell Jesse Romero to stop praying — it hurts, it hurts! Tell him to stop, or we're gonna hurt you!'" They said they would torment him the whole time I was praying for him, and then they threw him to the ground violently and twisted him like a pretzel into a painful position. He was screaming in pain that whole time, but then at just about 3:07 p.m., the demons suddenly let him go. He wanted to know when we had stopped praying, and yes, it was right at about 3:07 p.m.

Anita and I prayed for him at 3:00 p.m. every day for the next eight days, as I had promised. Each day, as soon as we had finished the Chaplet of Divine Mercy, he would call me right up. He was always hyperventilating and always told me the same thing: he was attacked by the demons inside of him the entire six or seven minutes that we prayed for him. And all through it, the demons would yell at him that he needed to make me stop, that our prayers were hurting them, and that they'd keep torturing him as long as he didn't make me stop. Those attacks happened every day for nine days straight, from 3:00 p.m. to 3:07 p.m.

Shortly after I finished my Divine Mercy novena for Abel, he was arrested for drunk driving, and he was deported to Mexico. I haven't seen him or heard from him since. While I don't know how things ended for him, or if he is still struggling with those same demons, I think of his story as a reminder that we Catholics have a power in our prayers. Whether vocal or mental, our prayers have an offensive nature to them, and they cause injury, torment, and pain to demons. Stay in a state of grace, and keep praying!

This was not the only time that I saw so clearly how demons are tormented by prayer. Once, when I was about to fly from Los Angeles to Dallas for a Catholic conference where I was scheduled to speak, I found myself standing behind a young man in the boarding line. As I waited, reading one of John Paul II's papal encyclicals, I noticed that the young man in front of me was looking at a porn magazine. He didn't make it hard to notice; he held it up proudly so that we could all see what he was "reading." The noises he was making while he looked at those pictures made it clear just how much enjoyment he was getting out of them, there in front of everyone.

I realized I felt sad for him; he clearly had no shame for what he was doing. Part of me wondered if maybe he was a baptized Catholic who had lost his way and was living in darkness. I decided I would say a quick, silent prayer for this guy and try to merit for him the grace of conversion. Because boy oh boy was he in a dark spot right then and there. In my mind, I offered a silent, heartfelt prayer for him, asking God to open the eyes of his heart, to grant him the grace of conversion, to bring him into relationship with the Lord Jesus Christ, and to protect him from any evil spirits that might be afflicting him.

As soon as I finished my prayer, he turned around quickly, looked right at me, and said with the angriest look I've ever seen, "Stop doing that. Stop it right now. I know what you're doing!"

I realized instantly that, somehow, he knew that I had offered a prayer for him — and this angered him immensely. How could he have known? I had prayed silently, mentally, all in my head. But what actually happened is that those demons who were clinging to him, directing him, and hovering over him were being tormented by my heartfelt intercessory prayer for him. They spoke to his *imagination* and *memory* (remember our five powers? and how the devils have access to all but the intellect and the will?) and convinced him to turn around, look at me, and rebuke me for praying for him.

This is one of those moments in my life that I'll always remember distinctly, a clear instance where I saw just how much prayer really is an offensive weapon that torments and injures demons.

You might be wondering, especially since I was praying in my head, if demons can hear silent prayers. Good question, and yes, they can, as you can tell from their reaction that day. This is because you can project prayers without actually speaking words out loud. Angels project knowledge without words as well: "Angels ... communicate by mental telepathy."[57] When you are praying in silent, meditative, or contemplative prayer, even though you are not speaking words out loud, you are still projecting prayers — God's words — into the cosmos. You are also projecting your emotions, and demons can detect these affections coming from your heart.

In a lighter example, we know that a husband and wife can communicate with each other without words. In a simple touch, a nod of the head, or a quick glance into each other's eyes, they can understand each other in a way that would take strangers a thousand words to explain. Unfortunately for us, demons are not stupid; way too much of the time, they can figure out what we're thinking, wishing, hoping, or fearing just by watching us. This nonverbal communication actually has a name, *kinesics*, which refers to movements and motions that we make with our body in a communicative nature. Simply put, it's our body language. In some professions, individuals have to be skilled at reading body language. Trained fighters and good policemen, for example, know how to read a person without words.

Like I said, demons are much more intelligent than we are, plus they study us all day long. St. Thomas Aquinas, whose reflections on angels earned him the title of "the Angelic Doctor," wrote concerning angels, "of the soul's powers only intellect and will can belong to them,"[58] and we know that demons all started out with that same angelic nature. Each demon that sets out to mislead us is like a dark actuary of human nature (an actuary is a person who computes premium rates, dividends, and risks according to probabilities based on statistical records). Demons can predict, based on a statistical

---

[57] Peter Kreeft, *Angels (and Demons): What Do We Really Know about Them?* (San Francisco: Ignatius Press, 1995), 65.

[58] St. Thomas Aquinas, *Summa Theologica* I, q. 54, art. 5.

probability they have devised by observing your pattern of behavior, what you will do in certain situations. Demons set up temptations specifically for you that they know you are specifically vulnerable to. They look at the pattern of your life and see if they can find a break, a weak spot. And if they find that break in your pattern, they will exploit it. But just as they can try to bring us to our knees without words, we can take the offensive, tormenting them with mental and all other kinds of prayer.

And take heart: demons are still far from omniscient. They can hear our prayers because we are projecting them into Heaven, and they can read and interpret our body language and past behaviors, but, as Fr. Fortea, an exorcist, says,

> Demons cannot read our thoughts. With their great intelligence, they can guess what we are thinking — but can never be absolutely certain. As spiritual beings, they are much more intelligent than we are, and as such, they can deduce things with greater accuracy and with fewer external signs than we can.… This being said, if one directs his mind and will to a saint, an angel, or a demon, they can hear us. So it does not matter whether our prayer is verbal or merely mental. In certain cases of possession, I have observed that the demon obeys orders that have been given mentally.[59]

Whether you are praying out loud or in your head, remember: your prayers can torment the demons who are attacking you or who are attacking the people you are praying for. Don't stop praying. Keep on the offensive.

---

[59]   Rev. Thomas J. Euteneuer, *Exorcism and the Church Militant* (Front Royal, VA: Human Life International, 2010), 177.

# CHAPTER 5

# Prayer: Protection from Demons

ON NOVEMBER 10, 2020, a Tuesday morning, I started the day with Mass, the Rosary, and two good Catholic friends, Bob and Armando, in Los Angeles. We needed fortification for the day ahead: we were going to spend the next two days investigating locations where satanism and witchcraft are practiced in the barrios of Los Angeles.

Bob Floyd is a Marine veteran, and Armando Valenzuela is a retired cop. Together, the three of us were out to help Bob on a project he had underway: compiling intelligence on practices of the occult. After receiving the spiritual armor we needed from Holy Mass and then arming ourselves with the Marian protection of the Rosary, we made our way to the Templo Santa Muerte, the "church" of the gang cult I talked about earlier, the demonic religion of the cartels that worships Satan.

The devotion to Santa Muerte is a gross mockery of Catholic devotions to real saints. She is not a real saint at all, and in fact her name means "holy death." In this occult following, death is personified by a skeleton with hair who is dressed in female grim reaper clothes and who carries a scythe and a globe. People who worship her think she'll bring them healing, protection, and safe delivery to the afterlife, but it is all a pack of satanic lies that trap people in demonic snares. The first Santa Muerte chapel was built by a female occultist, Enriqueta Romero (no relation to me), in Mexico City in 2001. Authentically Catholic Mexican bishops have unanimously condemned this demonic religion and have been so clear in their condemnation that they have said that Santa Muerte is in fact the devil himself.

As we parked our car and walked toward the entrance of the building, we could see that the two front doors were wide open. When we looked in, people were prostrate on the floor, with their buttocks in the air, worshipping Santa Muerte in unknown languages. The background in this "temple" was red and black. Maybe some of you remember when President Biden gave that polarizing speech to the nation on September 1, 2022, with that hellish red and black background.[60] It was just like that. But at least Biden was speaking in a language we could understand. On that day in Los Angeles, the satanic "parishioners" we saw worshipping inside were not speaking English, or Spanish, or Latin. They were speaking in diabolical tongues. Once you hear that kind of language, you can't unhear it. I turned to Bob and said to him, "Here we are. Go inside, take your pictures, and let's get out of this place." Bob just looked at me, and then he said, "I'm not going in there." Armando agreed with him.

But this was the last location on our checklist, and I was tired. I wanted to get back to the airport and fly home. So I told Bob, "Give me your camera. I will walk in there, snap a few pictures, and then we'll leave." I grabbed his camera, then I turned to walk through the open doors — but as soon as I stepped on the threshold, I felt these big hands push my chest. All at once, I flew back, tossed like a beach ball, into the arms of Bob and Armando. I said to myself, *what was*

---

[60]  Brian Flood, "Biden Shocks Viewers with 'Hellish Red Background' for Polarizing Speech," *Fox News*, September 2, 2022, https://www.foxnews.com/media/biden-shocks-viewers-hellish-red-background-polarizing-speech.

*that?* And I felt embarrassed. Looking back, I can see that my ego was bruised. I was angry that something could have thrown me around so easily. So I turned back, dead set on making it through that doorway — but again, I was pushed by some invisible hands on my chest, and I flew back. It felt like I had just run up against the Hulk. But even then, I was too stupid to understand the message that God was clearly trying to give me, and I swung back around for round three. When I tried to walk inside Templo Santa Muerte a third time, those invisible hands of steel hit my chest yet again, and I was thrown back like I'd just been speared by Bill Goldberg in a wrestling match.

Finally, and suddenly, I realized that my guardian angel, recognizing my stupidity, had pushed me out of that evil place on that Tuesday morning. My angel had my back at that shrine to the devil, that portal to Hell, that sits in the center of the City of the Angels — Los Angeles.

Bob and Armando's eyes were wide open in shock, and they both agreed that we should leave *right now*. Both of them told me afterward that it looked like I had hit an invisible force field at the threshold of this satanic temple, and that I was thrown back with incredible force every single time.

Here's the thing. I pray to my angel daily. In the morning, in the evening, and when I'm going to drive or get on a plane, I call upon my guardian angel. I didn't need to experience what I experienced on that November day in 2020 to believe that my guardian angel is real, but it was a really good reminder for me: angels are here to save us from demons, and even to save us from ourselves. Prayer helps us go on the offensive, for sure, and our angels give us defense when we get into situations, or put ourselves in situations, that are more than we can handle.

What does the Bible have to say about how the angels help us?

✠ "Are they not all ministering spirits sent forth to serve, for the sake of those who are to obtain salvation?" (Heb. 1:14). It is worth noting that in the original Greek, the word translated as "ministering," *leitourgika*, also means "given to the service of someone," or "for service."

✠ "The angel of the Lord encamps around those who fear him, and delivers them" (Ps. 34:7).

✠ "For he will give his angels charge of you to guard you in all your ways" (Ps. 91:11)

You'll notice when you put all of these verses together that angels serve us (the followers of Christ), they surround us, they guard us, and they deliver us from evil. We must call upon their help (see Matt. 7:7) if we want it in warding off demons, but they will always come when asked, because that is their ministry. Remember that St. Thomas Aquinas wrote that one of the roles of the guardian angels is to fight off demons.[61] And St. John Bosco is credited with saying: "When tempted, invoke your Angel. He is more eager to help you than you are to be helped! Ignore the devil and do not be afraid of him: He trembles and flees at the sight of your Guardian Angel." Unlike the angels, who must be called, demons are unfortunately always on hand, so we must constantly resist them.

When God put a calling on my life, he had already factored in my stupidity. And embarrassed as I might have been after that first smack down that day, knowing that God has already accounted for my stupidity is actually very comforting. And when I was thrown back into the arms of Bob Floyd and Armando Valenzuela, after I got what felt like a donkey kick to my chest from those invisible arms, I knew it was my guardian angel protecting my soul from entering into the

---

[61] St. Thomas Aquinas, *Summa Theologica* I, q. 113, arts. 2–6.

temple of Satan. My angel was protecting me from the possibility of becoming diabolically afflicted, which would have meant taking an evil spirit back home to my family.

*Angel of God, my Guardian dear …*

# When the Bullets Start Flying

In 1988, I traveled to Stockton, California, to compete in the California Police Olympics as part of the Los Angeles Sheriff's Department's boxing team. Anita was with me, and unfortunately, we had made our travel arrangements late; all we could find was a hotel on the rough side of town. A friend of mine, Danny, who was competing in wrestling, was also staying there, and so was his girlfriend. One night of the trip, all four of us were driving back to the hotel together, but we were not prepared for the scene that met us as we walked through that main entrance and into the lobby and found ourselves right in the middle of an armed robbery.

Four young men, with handguns out and ready, were robbing the hotel clerk, an older man. One robber was holding the victim by his shirt and was lifting him up in the air, about a foot off the ground. The others were robbing the cash box and going through all the desk drawers in search of more money. Their victim was clearly absolutely terrified and immobilized by fear. Lucky for us, the four thieves were so focused on their robbery that they didn't see us walk in. Danny and I were both carrying our weapons — I had a six-shot revolver, and Danny had a sixteen-shot semi-automatic Beretta pistol. We told the ladies to run straight to their rooms, call the Stockton Police Department, tell them about the robbery, and let them know that we were two armed off-duty sheriffs from LA who'd detain the robbers till the cops could get there.

There were two large, stone pillars in the lobby of the hotel. Danny stood behind one, I stood behind the other, and we looked at each other and signaled: *it's time*! We both yelled out, "You're under arrest! We're Los Angeles Deputy Sheriffs, and we're telling you to put your guns down NOW! You're under arrest — drop your guns and lie face down on the floor!" The four gang members were startled, but they didn't drop their guns. Instead, they looked at us, and then they raised their snub-nosed revolvers in our direction, doubling down on their wicked intentions. All six of us were pointing guns at each other, but the four of them were in the open lobby with no cover; Danny and I each had a huge stone pillar for cover.

I started mentally praying the Our Father and the Hail Mary in a loop as we were facing each other off. Suddenly, a 1965 Chevrolet Impala pulled up behind us, outside the hotel, with loud hip hop music coming from the speakers. We saw that the driver was a young guy, and we were sure he was the armed getaway driver. Danny and I looked at each other, and we both knew we were in real danger now: we now were looking at a crossfire situation, and we were off duty with no bullet-proof vests and no radios; we only had our service weapons and each other. But then, I heard the police sirens. The Stockton cops were on their way! So we both took out our badges, held them up over our heads, and continued to identify ourselves, telling them they were under arrest and to drop their weapons.

With all this commotion going on, people on the first floor of the hotel started coming out of their rooms to see what was going on. It's not every day you get a front-row seat to a violent confrontation between four gang members, two off-duty deputies, and a getaway driver waiting in the wings. As I turned to check on the driver behind us, I took my eyes off the other four suspects for a moment, and when I turned back, I realized I could only see three of them. One of them had moved on me, and I'd lost track of him while I was checking my six. But Danny had been visually and mentally locked in on all four of them the whole time, and he looked at me real quick and told me to duck. So I ducked, and Danny turned full toward me and fired a round right over my head, hitting the guy who had snuck around to my side right in his head. If Danny hadn't seen him and taken him out of commission, he would have shot me at close range on the left side of my head — and I would never have seen him coming. I started praying the St. Michael the Archangel prayer in a loop, going around on repeat in my head.

One suspect was down to my left, but there were still three of them in front of us and one behind us in the getaway car. I could hear the police sirens getting closer and closer, but then the three guys in front of us began firing their guns, shouting, "Booya, booya, booya!" — something some gang members yell out when they're firing at another person. And as they shot at us, they turned their guns horizontal. Sure, this is the "cool" way for someone to shoot a gun, but anyone who shoots sideways like that is going to miss his target by a country mile. We faced off with them and began unloading our weapons, and all the while I'm still mentally praying the St. Michael the Archangel prayer. Within just a few seconds, all three of them were hit several times and went down, but they kept firing their weapons until they were empty. The getaway driver could see what had happened and peeled off quickly, but he was stopped by the Stockton Police as he tried to exit the driveway of the hotel; he actually crashed into one of the patrol cars.

I asked God mentally to have mercy on all of us, especially these gang members. Many Stockton Police officers ran in with their weapons drawn, and that's when Danny and I put our weapons away and identified ourselves with our badges as Los Angeles Deputy Sheriffs.

We told them why we were in town and what we had walked into when we came back to the hotel after our evening's competition in the Police Olympics. We verified that we'd identified ourselves as law enforcement, that the suspects did not comply with our orders, and that an exchange of gunfire ensued, with the two of us firing because we feared for our lives, the life of the hotel clerk, and the lives of the other hotel guests on the first floor. When the cops interviewed several eyewitnesses, everybody — including the robbers who were still alive — corroborated our story.

And that's when the cops told us that these five suspects were notorious armed robbers. They were wanted for a rash of armed robberies in Stockton, and they'd originally come from the Crips street gang from south central Los Angeles. They had more recently moved to Stockton to start a new faction of the Crips. Finally, later that evening, we were told by the Stockton District Attorney's office and the Stockton Police homicide unit that our shooting was justified and within police policy. They took all of our information, we took a urine test, and they said we were free to leave.

The Stockton Police Department kept in touch with me and flew me back three months later to testify in court. One more suspect had died since the day of the robbery, and the three remaining men were there to stand trial for armed robbery and attempted murder against two law enforcement officers. They were convicted on all counts, and the judge sentenced all three of them to seventeen years to life. Once I was done testifying, the judge asked me right there in the court room, "Deputy Romero, is there something you would like to say to these defendants who tried to kill you?" "Certainly," I responded. I looked at the three defendants, who were all unfortunately in wheelchairs as a result of the injuries sustained during the shooting. I looked around the room and noted that the courtroom area for the general public was jam packed with their family and friends. As I turned back to the three of them, I said, "I hope and pray that when you three young men enter your place of imprisonment, that you open your hearts to God and surrender your lives to God. I hope He creates in you a pure, clean heart, and that you all discover the meaning and purpose of life according to God's plan for you. I harbor no resentment, bitterness, or ill feelings toward any of you."

I got up and stepped down from the witness stand, but the judge said "Deputy Romero, stop there." I thought, "Oh no, I pissed off the judge, what did I say that upset him." But he surprised me again. "I have been in this courtroom for twenty years," he said, "and I have never heard a law enforcement officer speak such measured, tempered, and kind words to someone who tried to shoot him. I hope the Los Angeles Sheriff's Department has a thousand deputies with your demeanor and character. You may go now." And as I walked out of the courtroom, through the family and friends of the defendants, I thanked God for the opportunity to share my faith with a courtroom full of people that day. And I thanked him for the prayers that had risen in my head that day in Stockton, the prayers that had kept us safe when we were unprepared and outnumbered, and the bullets were flying around us.

# Rosary in the Breach: Antifa and St. Junípero Serra

ON JUNE 25, 2020, my younger brother, Johnny Romero, received a call from a fellow pro-life Catholic, Laura Chavez. She told him that Black Lives Matter (BLM) and Antifa activists were on their way to San Fernando Mission Park, across from the Catholic Mission, in the city of Mission Hills, California. About a hundred anarchists were marching over there to tear down a statue of St. Junípero Serra, the great Catholic missionary who evangelized and brought Catholic culture to the pagan indigenous people in California. Johnny is a former Marine and a blue-collar worker at the LA Department of Water and Power. He is also a father of six children, all of whom he raised to be zealous Catholics, just like he is. He is exactly the sort of no-nonsense, hardcore, devout man you want on your side if you're thinking it's time to take on the mob.

God chose and ordained that the spiritual foundations of California, from the time of the Age of Exploration and onward, would be Spanish, Franciscan, and Catholic. What Catholicism has built in California is a continuous and unbroken chain of tradition that goes all the way back through Mexico and Spain to Christ. In California, all the twenty-one historical Spanish missions and various mountains, rivers, valleys, points along the coast, cities, and freeways are named after Catholic saints. Los Angeles, for example, was given its name by Fr. Crespi in 1789, when he called it "the town of Our Lady, Queen of the Angels."[62]

My brother Johnny knows and loves all of this rich history, so, without hesitating, and because of his love for God and our Catholic religion, he answered Laura's call. He drove over to the San Fernando Mission Park, armed with a rosary, and met up with six other Catholic men who were also called to be there. They exited their cars and ran over to stand in front of the statue of St. Junípero Serra, although they could see a mob of well over a hundred anarchists coming toward them. Johnny and these six other Catholic men all stood in a fighting stance — left feet forward, right feet back — and began praying the Rosary. When the mob came up to them, Johnny and the other men stood their ground, prayed, and ordered them: "Back off. You're not destroying this statue." And these seven men (coincidentally, seven is known as both the perfect number and the number of God) held back more than a hundred BLM and Antifa anarchists, many of whom were armed with chains, and all of them hell-bent on toppling the statue of this great Catholic saint. The mob was screaming, cussing, and threatening them with violence, saying they'd take them down if they didn't move out of the way.

The Los Angeles Police Department finally arrived with a few patrol cars. The officers who showed up were visibly afraid as they stood with my brother and his friends on one side and the angry, threatening mob on the other. Someone who was there was taking a video on his phone, and he sent me the whole showdown. The police started by asking my brother and the other Catholic men to please

---

[62] "Where Did the Name 'Los Angeles' Come From?" *Los Angeles Almanac,* https://laalmanac.com/history/hi03a.php.

leave and to allow the mob to take down the statues. But Johnny stood up to the police. He told them, respectfully, that they must do their job. They must defend this piece of historical property from vandalism. And if they did not do their job, Johnny said, he and his friends would be forced to do it for them. Long and short: Johnny stood his ground, in front of the police *and* in front of the mob.

When the police saw my brother's tenacity, they drew courage from him and his six friends. They stepped up and decided to do the right thing. They told the mob that they must leave because they were "unlawfully assembling to commit a property crime." Little by little, the mob began to realize that my brother and his friends were not backing down, and then they saw that the police were now on my brother's side — the side of law and order. And so the mob began to disperse, and, as they left, my brother and the six men who were with him continued to hold their rosaries out like weapons in front of them, praying to the Queen of Heaven for her mantle of protection.

What's the lesson to be learned here? My brother did not hesitate to go protect that statue of St. Junípero Serra. He didn't wait for someone to give him permission. He did what he knew was the right and courageous thing out of his love for God and for the Catholic Faith. Natural law and his Catholic Faith compelled him to put his body in harm's way, to stand in front of that statue and in front of a mob that had real bad intentions. When I talked to him about it later, he said he realized in retrospect that he could have been killed, could have left his six kids without a dad. But even so, he said, he felt duty-bound by his Catholic Faith to go into the public square, defend a statue of the Church, and suffer the consequences. He and those six other Catholic men were willing to take up space for Jesus and "stand in the breach" (Ezek. 22:30), all for the purpose of sanctifying the public square by a witness of faith and by prayers of supplication and petition to the Virgin Most Powerful.

# Chapter 8

# At the Hour of Our Death

I ONCE KNEW A priest with whom I shared a close friendship. Over the years, we had participated together in various ministries. He had visited my family, and he had provided sacraments to our children and to Anita and myself. When he would come to visit, Anita remarked once or twice that he and I seemed to be such close friends, that we clearly liked and respected each other, but she always felt as if she were invisible to him. Although I heard what she was saying, I honestly never thought too much about it, other than acknowledging that she felt slighted by him. But he and I would visit and talk for hours about God, theology, Scripture, religion, and history. One day, he said to me, very sadly, "I wish I had faith like you have." Anita overheard him, and she talked to me about it afterward, letting me know that she found it very disturbing that a Catholic priest would say that to a nobody lay person like me. Shouldn't a priest have much stronger faith than one of us? But, once again, I did not think much of her concern.

Time passed, and I realized that it had been quite a while since I'd seen this priest at his regular Masses. When I asked one of his brother priests where he was, he said he had gotten very sick and was close to death, and that he'd be asking all of his congregations to pray for him at each Mass. And now, like Anita, I felt like something wasn't sitting right. It wasn't that long ago that I'd seen him, and it was hard to imagine that anyone could get that sick that quickly — and it was especially troubling that he hadn't talked to me about it at all before he left, as we had developed a good friendship. Something didn't seem right, but I went ahead and joined the community in praying for him. And each week, I made an attempt to get in touch with him, but I could never get through, and he did not respond.

Something was fishy, but I just kept him in my thoughts and occasionally prayed for him. Finally, one day, I got a call at home. My friend was asking to see me after all this time, and he wanted to know if I could come that very day. I jumped in the car right away, calculating that I had about four hours to visit before work started. I would see what I could do to help. I wanted to be there for my friend.

A housekeeper greeted me when I rang the bell, and she brought me down the hall to a closed door, then motioned for me to go in on my own. Quietly, I cracked it open, then stepped into the room. I saw my dear friend lying on a bed, and he looked like a skeleton, all skin and bones. He was a tall man, six foot four, and now his height made him look even thinner. I ran toward him, bent down, and embraced him chest to chest in fraternal Christian love.

We were both teary eyed. I told him how much I had missed him and asked why he hadn't called me. He told me that he was embarrassed, so I said, "Why would you be embarrassed about being sick? That's nothing to be embarrassed about." Then, suddenly, I had a lightbulb go off in my head, like the Holy Spirit was giving me a revelation. "Father," I said slowly, "You're not just sick.... You're dying of AIDS, aren't you?" He looked at me, and he nodded. "Yes," he answered simply, "I have AIDS." I was brokenhearted to hear this, but I still reserved judgment — until he launched into a tirade against Holy Mother Church.

"The Church is wrong about homosexuality," he said. Then he started speaking more quickly, and with anger. "The Church must change her teachings. She has to catch up with the times, and I *disagree* with the Church's teachings on homosexuality." I was appalled to hear a Catholic priest speak heresies so boldly, especially as he was lying there literally so sick with AIDS that he was dying. His present physical condition was proof positive that he was wrong about the consequences of homosexual sex. And that's when I lost my cool for a second, and I yelled at him, saying, "No, Father, you're wrong, the Church is right, and you better repent right now. You are *dying*, and I refuse to let a friend of mine go to Hell. You must repent and confess your sins *now*, before it's too late. I will not let you go to Hell!" At this point we were both screaming at each other, face to face, like two boxers at a press conference before a fight. He could smell my hot breath, and I could smell his. I even grabbed him by the t-shirt and shook him like a rag doll, insisting, "*No*, Father, you're wrong. Repent! Please, repent."

Looking at his stubbornness in this moment, I knew I was witnessing the power of sexual sin and its blinding effect, even on a Catholic priest who had been providing the sacraments to my family and me for years. It was a powerful and terrible thing to see.

But that was not the end of his story. When we both finally calmed down and took a beat, he looked at me, then shook his head and started to cry. "The real reason I called you," he said, "was that I knew you were the only person who would tell the truth and set me straight. I know you're right." At this, I embraced him again, with all the true affection I held for him, and he returned the same brotherly affection. "Okay," he said. "Go get me a priest." And so I did, right then and there, and then I paced up and down the hallway as he made his last confession, praying the Rosary for his conversion and joining my prayers to the prayers of everyone who had been praying for him during his months of illness. By the time I finished praying the Rosary, the other priest walked out of the room, looked at me, and gave me a thumbs up. "It's taken care of," he said with a smile. "It's done." My friend had confessed his sins.

I walked back into his room and exclaimed to him how happy I was for him, how proud I was of him. It takes a real man to own up to his sins. I told him, since he was obviously going to die before me, that I wanted him to kiss Jesus and Mary for me. And I also told him to give Venerable Fulton Sheen a big holy hug and an immense thank you from me since I was learning so much through his books and cassette tapes. Last of all, I told him, "When the day comes that the Lord takes you home, save a spot in God's Kingdom for me."

I went straight from there to work that evening, my head still spinning from all the drama of such an intense episode. The next morning, I received another phone call: my friend, the priest, had died just a few hours earlier. The news was bittersweet, but it was not surprising. He was just like the good thief on the cross next to Jesus, St. Dismas; he had stolen his salvation at the very end. "Though your sins are like scarlet they shall be as white as snow" (Isa. 1:18). He had lost his way as a priest and had fallen victim to the culture of death — and he had paid the physical consequences of his sin, cutting his life short. However, despite all this, at the end of his life, the truth had set him free (John 8:32), and his soul was saved from eternal damnation. Thank You, Jesus; thank You for Your amazing grace and divine mercy!

After reading this, hopefully you now understand why I stand by our Holy Mother Church and her teachings. Secular catchphrases like "love wins" and "love is love" make homosexual relationships seem innocent and harmless. But regardless of such happy-sounding slogans, the fact is that men who have sex with men make up a disproportionate majority of HIV diagnoses and HIV- or AIDS-related deaths each year. Look up any government website on HIV and AIDS, and you'll see that they all say the same thing: about 2 to 4 percent of the United States population is made up of bisexual and homosexual men,[63] but homosexual and bisexual men make up about 70 percent of new HIV diagnoses in the United States each year — *70 percent!*[64] And while improved treatment for HIV and AIDS is overall extending people's lives, according to the CDC, a total of 4,941 people with HIV still died in 2022.[65] Encouraging homosexual sex promotes a culture of death.

My priest friend had a whole army of people praying for him in the last weeks of his life, and these people, knowingly or unknowingly, provided a complete arsenal of weapons to help him stand against the gates of Hell at the hour of his death. But how many souls does our culture of death abandon to eternal damnation, without hope of any help at all?

[63]   Jeffrey M. Jones, "U.S. LGBT Identification Steady at 7.2%," *Gallup*, February 22, 2023, https://news.gallup.com/poll/470708/lgbt-identification-steady.aspx.

[64]   "Fast Facts: HIV and Gay and Bisexual Men," *Centers for Disease Control and Prevention*, April 24, 2024, https://www.cdc.gov/hiv/data-research/facts-stats/gay-bisexual-men.html?CDC_AAref_Val=https://www.cdc.gov/hiv/group/msm/index.html.

[65]   "AIDS and HIV," *Centers for Disease Control and Prevention*, April 20, 2024, https://www.cdc.gov/nchs/fastats/aids-hiv.htm.

# Part III

# Annotated Quotations

OVER THE CENTURIES, WRITERS across all generations and in every age have written about prayer, spiritual warfare, and how we can prepare ourselves to join in the fight against the gates of Hell. I've thought a lot about this fight. In the earlier sections of this book, I've shared with you some of the ideas and particular experiences that have helped me to understand this conflict in practice. I hope that my words, and my encounters with angels, demons, and the grace of God, will help you as the Lord trains your hands for war and your fingers for battle.

What else can help you? In the following pages, in this third section of my book, I've compiled a lot of quotations from the Catechism, from Scripture and Tradition, and from modern Catholic thinkers. Starting with a deep dive into sacramentals, all of these quotations are organized into various ideas or themes that can increase your understanding of the spiritual battlefield. After you are done reading this book, I hope that you will return to this section from time to time. When you need encouragement in the fight, when you need a reminder of the reality of what we're up against and a reminder of how to arm yourself to take it on, look at the chapters below to find what you need. Spend some time meditating and praying over the words of Scripture, the writings of the saints, and the contributions of insightful Catholics.

Just like in the rest of this book, except where noted as something else, the Scripture translation I'm using is the Revised Standard Version Catholic Edition. I will sometimes also provide, *in italics*, some commentary on the words quoted below. But mostly I will just let the words speak for themselves.

Love God, save souls, slay error! And may God be with you in the fight.

# Chapter 1

# An Arsenal of Sacramentals

*Sacramentals are powerful weapons that God has given to us to help fight the good fight in the conflict of spiritual warfare. They bring us grace in a variety of ways through prayers and holy objects that strengthen us, heal us, and bring us closer to God. In this chapter, I will share some great quotations from various sources to illustrate some of the key points about sacramentals in general: what they are, and what they can do for us. In a few spots, I'll add some commentary to help you chew on the heavier stuff. Then, at the end of this chapter, I'll also talk about some particular sacramentals, such as holy water and saints' medals, to show you how they are helpful individually.*

## Catechism of the Catholic Church on Sacramentals

✠ CCC 1667: Holy Mother Church has, moreover, instituted sacramentals. These are sacred signs which bear a resemblance to the sacraments. They signify effects, particularly of a spiritual nature, which are obtained through the intercession of the Church. By them men are disposed to receive the chief effect of the sacraments, and various occasions in life are rendered holy.

✠ CCC 1668: Sacramentals are instituted for the sanctification of certain ministries of the Church, certain states of life, a great variety of circumstances in Christian life, and the use of many things helpful to man. In accordance with bishops' pastoral decisions, they can also respond to the needs, culture, and special history of the Christian people of a particular region or time. They always include a prayer, often accompanied by a specific sign, such as the laying on of hands, the sign of the cross, or the sprinkling of holy water (which recalls Baptism).

✠ CCC 1669: Sacramentals derive from the baptismal priesthood: every baptized person is called to be a "blessing," and to bless. Hence laypeople may preside at certain blessings; the more a blessing concerns ecclesial and sacramental life, the more is its administration reserved to the ordained ministry (bishops, priests, or deacons).

✠ CCC 1670: Sacramentals do not confer the grace of the Holy Spirit in the way that the sacraments do, but by the Church's prayer, they prepare us to receive grace and dispose us to cooperate with it. "For well-disposed members of the faithful, the liturgy of the sacraments and sacramentals sanctifies almost every event of their lives with the divine grace which flows from the Paschal mystery of the Passion, Death and Resurrection of Christ. From this source all sacraments and sacramentals draw their power. There is scarcely any proper use of material things which cannot be thus directed toward the sanctification of men and the praise of God."

## Sacramentals and Popular Piety

✠ CCC 1674: Besides sacramental liturgy and sacramentals, catechesis must take into account the forms of piety and popular devotions among the faithful. The religious sense of the Christian people has always found expression in various forms of piety surrounding the Church's sacramental life, such as the veneration of relics, visits to sanctuaries, pilgrimages, processions, the Stations of the Cross, religious dances, the rosary, medals, etc.

✠ CCC 1675: These expressions of piety extend the liturgical life of the Church, but do not replace it. They "should be so drawn up that they harmonize with the liturgical seasons, accord with the sacred liturgy, are in some way derived from it and lead the people to it, since in fact the liturgy by its very nature is far superior to any of them."

✠ "The sacramentals of themselves do not remit venial sins, but they move us to truer devotion, to greater love for God, and greater sorrow for our sins, and this devotion, love, and sorrow bring us grace, and the grace remits venial sins."[66]

## Various Forms of Sacramentals

### Exorcism

✠ CCC 1673: When the Church asks publicly and authoritatively in the name of Jesus Christ that a person or object be protected against the power of the Evil One and withdrawn from his dominion, it is called exorcism. Jesus performed

---

[66] *Baltimore Catechism*, no. 2, q. 1054.

exorcisms and from him the Church has received the power and office of exorcizing. In a simple form, exorcism is performed at the celebration of Baptism. The solemn exorcism, called "a major exorcism," can be performed only by a priest and with the permission of the bishop. The priest must proceed with prudence, strictly observing the rules established by the Church. Exorcism is directed at the expulsion of demons or to the liberation from demonic possession through the spiritual authority which Jesus entrusted to his Church. Illness, especially psychological illness, is a very different matter; treating this is the concern of medical science. Therefore, before an exorcism is performed, it is important to ascertain that one is dealing with the presence of the Evil One, and not an illness.

*As we discussed in the first chapter, only priests and bishops may perform major exorcisms, and even then only with permission. Additionally, there is a special book,* Manual of Minor Exorcisms: For the Use of Priests, *that every priest should have in his toolbox. Laypeople may also pray some prayers of minor exorcism; as noted earlier, when in doubt about which deliverance prayers we have the authority to pray, we can always ask a good priest for guidance. If you're looking for a safe place to start, here are some suggestions, prayers that I recommend be prayed daily by all Catholics: the prayers of the* Auxilium Christianorum *(lengthy prayers for each day of the week, available online at auxiliumchristianorum.org); Psalm 91; the Prayer for Deliverance from Evil; the Prayer to St. Joseph, Terror of Demons; Beneath Thy Protection; the Exorcism Prayers of the St. Benedict Medal; and the Exorcism Prayer of St. Anthony. I've included most of these for your reference in the section at the back of this book.*

## Holy Water

*As a sacramental, holy water remits venial sin. Every Catholic home should have a supply of it for healing, spiritual cleansing and protection from the devil and his cronies. In fact, it is so powerful that the poor souls in purgatory long for it, knowing what it could do for them. Consider the following words from Archbishop Albert G. Meyer in his 1958 pamphlet, "Holy Water: A Means of Spiritual Wealth."*[67]

⊹ "Because of the blessing attached to it, Holy Church strongly urges its use upon her children, especially when dangers threaten, such as fire, storms, sickness, and other calamities."

⊹ "The devil hates holy water because of its power over him. He cannot long abide in a place or near a person that is often sprinkled with this blessed water."

⊹ "Holy water, sprinkled with faith and piety, can move the Sacred Heart to bless your loved ones and protect them from all harm of soul and body."

⊹ "Only in Purgatory can one understand how ardently a poor soul longs for holy water. The holy souls nearest to Heaven may need the sprinkling of only one drop to relieve their pining souls."

*In her autobiography, St. Teresa of Ávila, a Doctor of the Church, relates a tale that demonstrates in a terrifying way just how powerful holy water is in our defense against the devil. Reading her account makes it pretty clear how powerful this simple gift is — and it's something we can keep in our homes, on our bedside tables, by our doors, and use multiple times a*

[67]  "Holy Water: A Means of Spiritual Wealth," pamphlet, imprimatur Albert G. Meyer, Archbishop of Milwaukee (January 13, 1958); quoted in "Holy Water," *Holy Reflections*, https://www.holyreflections.com/holywater.html.

*day, coming and going, sleeping and waking, to bless and protect ourselves and our children against the forces of the devil:*

> Once, when I was in an oratory, he appeared on my left hand in an abominable form; as he spoke to me, I paid particular attention to his mouth, which was horrible. Out of his body there seemed to be coming a great flame, which was intensely bright and cast no shadow. He told me in a horrible way that I had indeed escaped out of his hands but he would get hold of me still. I was very much afraid and made the sign of the cross as well as I could, whereupon he disappeared, but immediately returned again. This happened twice running and I did not know what to do. But there was some holy water there, so I flung some in the direction of the apparition, and it never came back.... From long experience I have learned that there is nothing like holy water to put devils to flight and prevent them from coming back again.[68]

*Following in St. Teresa's spiritual footsteps in Colombia in 2019, one Catholic bishop admirably demonstrated how much faith he puts in this simple sacramental when he borrowed a helicopter from the navy. He could see the extent to which demons were tormenting the people who lived in his town, and he determined that it was time to do something concrete about it. He got in that helicopter, and he sprayed the entire city with holy water.[69]*

---

[68]   St. Teresa of Ávila, *The Life of Teresa of Jesus*, trans. and ed. E. Allison Peers, 173; available at https://www.carmelitemonks.org/Vocation/teresa_life.pdf.

[69]   Daniel Avery, "Bishop Plans to Spray City with Holy Water from Helicopter: 'We Have to Get Rid of the Devil,'" *Newsweek*, June 25, 2019, https://www.newsweek.com/bishop-holy-water-helicopter-1445828.

*Even in the Old Testament, Scripture gives us an understanding of the existence of and the power of holy water:*

✠ "And the priest shall take holy water in an earthen vessel, and take some of the dust that is on the floor of the tabernacle and put it into the water" (Num. 5:17).

✠ "And Eli'sha sent a messenger to him, saying, "Go and wash in the Jordan seven times, and your flesh shall be restored, and you shall be clean." But Na'aman was angry, and went away, saying, "Behold, I thought that he would surely come out to me, and stand, and call on the name of the Lord his God, and wave his hand over the place, and cure the leper. Are not Aba'na and Pharpar, the rivers of Damascus, better than all the waters of Israel? Could I not wash in them, and be clean?" So he turned and went away in a rage. But his servants came near and said to him, "My father, if the prophet had commanded you to do some great thing, would you not have done it? How much rather, then, when he says to you, 'Wash, and be clean'?" So he went down and dipped himself seven times in the Jordan, according to the word of the man of God; and his flesh was restored like the flesh of a little child, and he was clean" (2 Kings 5:10–14).

*When a priest blesses the water, that is, when he makes holy water, he prays the following prayer. You can see in the words of this prayer just what it does for us, what an effective weapon it is for us:*

"O God, grant that this creature of Thine (water) may be endowed with divine grace to drive away devils and to cast out diseases, that whatever in the houses or possessions of the faithful may be sprinkled by this water, may be freed from everything unclean, and delivered from

what is hurtful. . . . Let everything that threatens the safety
or peace of the dwellers therein be banished by the sprinkling of this water; so that the health which they seek by
calling upon Thy Holy Name may be guarded from all
assault."

*When we bless ourselves with holy water, we can pray a simple prayer to
increase its efficacy in our lives:*

"By this Holy Water and by Thy Precious Blood, cleanse
me from my sins, O Lord."

## Blessed Salt

*Blessed salt can be used to help keep us from sin, sickness, or demonic influ-
ence. We can use modest amounts of blessed salt to bless and protect our
homes, our cars, or ourselves.[70] A few grains of blessed salt in drinking
water or used in cooking or as food seasoning often bring astonishing spiritual and physical benefits. Any amount of salt may be presented to a priest
for his blessing.[71] Do not be shy about asking a priest to use the blessing
(for salt or anything else) from the old* Roman Ritual *rather than the
newer* Book of Blessings. *The older blessing is included here. As Fr. Ralph
Weimann demonstrates repeatedly throughout his authoritative book on
sacramentals, the prayers and blessings in the* Roman Ritual *are both*

---

[70]  Fr. Gabriele Amorth, " 'The Devil Is Real': Insights on Spiritual Warfare from Fr. Gabriele Amorth," *The Catholic Exchange*, May 15, 2020,
https://catholicexchange.com/the-devil-is-real-insights-on-spiritual-
warfare-from-fr-gabriele-amorth/.

[71]  "Blessed Salt," *CatholicSacramentals.org*, https://www.catholicsacramen-
tals.org/blessed-salt.

*much more powerful and more specific than those included in the* Book of Blessings.[72]

Exorcism of Salt (necessary for the Exorcism of Water)
(Priest vests in surplice and purple stole)

P: Our help is in the Name of the Lord.
R: Who made Heaven and earth.

P: O salt, creature of God, I exorcise you by the living (+) God, by the true (+) God, by the holy (+) God, by the God who ordered you to be poured into the water by Elisha the prophet, so that its life-giving powers might be restored. I exorcise you so that you may become a means of salvation for believers, that you may bring health of soul and body to all who make use of you, and that you may put to flight and drive away from the places where you are sprinkled; every apparition, villainy, turn of devilish deceit, and every unclean spirit; adjured by him who will come to judge the living and the dead and the world by fire.

R: Amen.

P: Let us pray. Almighty and everlasting God, we humbly implore You, in Your immeasurable kindness and love, to bless (+) this salt which You created and gave to the use of mankind, so that it may become a source of health for the minds and bodies of all who make use of it. May it rid whatever it touches or sprinkles of all uncleanness, and protect it from every assault of evil spirits. Through Christ our Lord.

R: Amen.

---

[72]  Fr. Ralph Weiman, *Sacramentals: Their Meaning and Spiritual Use* (Nashua, NH: Sophia Institute Press, 2023).

*Multiple priests and layman who are either well-practiced in exorcisms or who have studied and assisted in them also have a lot to say about the power of blessed salt:*

- ✠ "Part of the healing to remove generational curses is to put blessed salt on your food."[73]

- ✠ "Blessed salt on the outside perimeter of your property (office space, hotel room) is also very effective if the house is infested with demons. They have an aversion to blessed salt."[74]

- ✠ "It can be sprinkled in corners and over door jambs because it tends to remain where it is placed. It can be used for cooking and medicinal purposes."

### The Miraculous Medal

*St. Maximilian Kolbe said that the Miraculous Medal is a spiritual bullet in the war to win souls. With this bullet, he said, the faithful soldier hits the evil enemy and rescues souls.[75] The physical appearance of the medal was proscribed by Mary herself:*

> In a vision, Mary stood on a globe, with brilliant light streaming from her jeweled fingers. "Behold the symbol of graces shed upon those who ask for them," she said, representing herself as Mediatrix of All Graces. Surrounding her was a banner which read, "O Mary, conceived without sin,

---

[73] Dr. Dan Schneider, unpublished essay, "Evidence of Familial Generational Curses."

[74] Dr. Dan Schneider, unpublished essay, "Spiritual Warfare in Haunted Houses."

[75] Quoted in Linda O'Brien, "That Wondrous Miraculous Medal of the Immaculate Conception," *Catholic Exchange*, November 26, 2007, https://catholicexchange.com/that-wondrous-miraculous-medal-of-the-immaculate-conception/.

pray for us who have recourse to thee," symbolizing her Immaculate Conception. The vision reversed, showing the letter 'M' entwined with a cross above the Sacred Hearts. This image represents Mary as co-redemptrix, a unique participator in Jesus' saving act of redemption. Millions of medals have been distributed and untold graces given "to those who wear it around the neck" as the Virgin promised to St. Catherine.[76]

*One of my favorite stories about the Miraculous Medal is about an agnostic man in the 1800s, Alphonse Ratisbonne. He hated the Catholic Church, mostly because his older brother had left their wealthy Jewish family to become a Catholic priest. But then one of his brother's Catholic friends, Baron Thèodore de Bussières, gave Alphonse a Miraculous Medal. Shortly after, Alphonse accompanied the baron to a local church where a funeral for one of the baron's friends was being prepared. The baron left Alphonse for a moment, and when he returned, he saw Alphonse on his knees, weeping:[77]*

I had been but a few moments in the church when I was suddenly seized with an unutterable agitation of mind. I raised my eyes, the building had disappeared from before me; one single chapel had, so to speak, gathered and concentrated all the light; and in the midst of this radiance I saw standing on the altar, lofty, clothed with splendors, full of majesty and of sweetness, the Virgin Mary, just as she is represented on my medal. An irresistible force drew me towards her: the Virgin made me a sign with her hand

[76]  "About the Miraculous Medal," *Catholic Saint Medals*, https://catholic-saintmedals.com/about-the-miraculous-medal/.

[77]  Armando Santos, "The Conversion of Alphonse Ratisbonne," *The American Society for the Defense of Tradition, Family, and Property*, November 2, 2015, https://www.tfp.org/the-conversion-of-alphonse-ratisbonne/.

> that I should kneel down; and then she seemed to say,
> That will do! She spoke not a word, but I understood all.[78]

*In the end, Alphonse became a Catholic priest, just like his brother. Later, St. Maximilian Kolbe heard his story, and he became convinced of the power of the Miraculous Medal. When he started the Militia of the Immaculata — the Army of the Immaculate One — in 1917, wearing and giving away Miraculous Medals was a big part of their work.*

*Another powerful story is about twenty-year-old Claude Newman. In 1943, he was sitting on death row in a Mississippi prison. He had shot Sid Cook, his grandmother's abusive second husband. While he was in prison, he noticed a medal hanging around the neck of another prisoner, and he asked him what it was. The other guy ripped it off his neck, threw it on the ground, and told him to take it if he wanted it. Claude still didn't know what it was, but he picked it up and hung it around his neck. It was, of course, the Miraculous Medal. That simple action changed his whole existence: that night, Our Lady appeared to Claude. Claude summoned a priest the next day, began his catechesis, and soon converted to the Catholic Faith. When the day came for his execution, he went to his death joyfully, as he knew his soul was saved because of the Miraculous Medal.[79]*

### The Brown Scapular of Our Lady of Mount Carmel

*The brown scapular is worn around the neck. We received it through St. Simon Stock, an English Carmelite priest, when Our Lady appeared to him in the thirteenth century and gave it to him. She promised that anyone who dies wearing a scapular will not go to Hell. Since then, it has always*

---

[78]  Baron Thèodore de Bussières, *The Conversion of M. Marie-Alphonse Ratisbonne*, ed. Rev. W. Lockhart (London: Burns and Oates), 11–12.

[79]  Andrea Phillips, "A Medal, a Vision, a Conversion — the Story of Claude Newman," *The American Society for the Defense of Tradition, Family, and Property*, November 12, 2015, https://www.tfp.org/a-medal-a-vision-a-conversion-the-story-of-claude-newman/.

*been associated with the Carmelite religious order; and most scapulars today are even made out of the wool of Carmelite habits. One Carmelite community writes:*

> One of the signs in the tradition of the Church from many centuries ago is the Brown Scapular of Our Lady of Mount Carmel. It is a spiritual sign approved by the Church and accepted by the Carmelite Order as "an external sign of love for Mary, of the trust her children have in her, and of a commitment to live like her." The scapular finds its roots in the tradition of the Order, which has seen in it a sign of Mary's motherly protection.... It stands for a commitment to follow Jesus, like Mary, the perfect model of all the disciples of Christ. This commitment finds its origin in Baptism by which we become children of God.... It is an expression of our belief that we will meet God in eternal life, aided by the intercession and prayers of Mary.[80]

*The scapular helps us to live authentic Christian lives in line with the gospel. It helps us to go to the sacraments often, and it also helps us to profess our special devotion to the Blessed Virgin, something that we should do at least three times a day, for example, by saying a Hail Mary. We shouldn't take the promise of the brown scapular — that we won't go to Hell if we're wearing it — as some sort of superstition:*

> This must not be understood superstitiously or magically, but in light of Catholic teaching that perseverance in faith, hope and love are required for salvation. The scapular is a

---

[80]  "The Brown Scapular," *The Carmelites: Australia and Timor-Leste*, accessed May 4, 2024, https://www.carmelites.org.au/prayer-reflections/the-brown-scapular.

powerful reminder of this Christian obligation and of Mary's promise to help those consecrated to her obtain the grace of final perseverance.[81]

*Writer John Henderson of OnePeterFive talks about another promise that comes with this sacramental:*

In addition to the promise to be saved from Hell, there is another major brown scapular privilege, the Sabbatine Privilege, which was first made known in a bull written by Pope John XXII in 1322. Pope Paul V also composed a decree on the Sabbatine Privilege in which he wrote, "The Blessed Virgin will assist by her continual intercession, suffrages and merits, and also by her special protection, particularly on the Saturday after death, the souls of the members of the [Scapular] Confraternity departing this life in charity who shall have worn the scapular, observed chastity according to their particular state of life, and also have recited the Little Office, and have abstained from the use of meat on Wednesdays and Saturdays. The Sabbatine Privilege has been explicitly confirmed by Clement VII, St. Pius V, Gregory XIII, Paul V, and St. Pius X. St. John of the Cross was referring to his hope in this privilege when he told his brothers that he would consider it a great grace from Our Lady to die on a Saturday.[82]

---

[81]  "Brown Scapular or Scapular of Our Lady of Mount Carmel," *Veil of Innocence*, accessed May 4, 2024, https://veilofinnocence.org/prayer/sacpula-promises-of-our-lady/.

[82]  John Henderson, "The Brown Scapular and the Sabbatine Privilege," *OnePeterFive*, July 15, 2021, https://onepeterfive.com/the-brown-scapular-and-the-sabbatine-privilege/.

*For one final comment on the grace that comes to us through this sacramental, specifically its use as a weapon against demonic forces, look at this:*

> Throughout history it has aided a countless number of Christian souls and has proven to be a powerful defense against Satan. In the booklet *Garment of Grace*, evidence for this claim is found in the life of Venerable Francis Ypes. According to the story, "One day his Scapular fell off. As he replaced it, the devil howled, 'Take off the habit which snatches so many souls from us!' Then and there, Francis made the devil admit that there are three things which the demons are most afraid of: the Holy Name of Jesus, the Holy Name of Mary, and the Holy Scapular of Carmel.... Consequently, when the wearing of a Brown Scapular leads a person to develop a "habit" of faith, it becomes a strong defense against Satan as it draws a person closer to the Virgin Mary, whom the devil vehemently abhors.[83]

## THE ST. BENEDICT MEDAL

*The St. Benedict Medal is a two-sided medal that has a picture of St. Benedict on one side and a cross on the other. On the back of the medal, around the sides and along the cross, there are the initials of two Latin exorcism prayers, explained in further detail in the description below. Because of these prayers, wearing this medal gives you an especially powerful defense against demonic attack. In fact, the St. Benedict Medal is the only medal in the Church that has an exorcism prayer placed on it, and the St. Benedict crucifix is the official crucifix used by Catholic priests during*

---

[83] Philip Kosloski, "This Is Why Satan Hates the Brown Scapular," *Aleteia*, July 16, 2018.

*exorcisms. Once again, the Carmelites can tell us a lot about sacramentals. One of their communities of sisters has written a lengthy description and explanation of this medal:*

> **Use of the Medal:** There is no special way prescribed for carrying or wearing the Medal of St. Benedict. It can be worn on a chain around the neck, attached to one's rosary, kept in one's pocket or purse, or placed in one's car or home. The medal is often put into the foundations of houses and buildings, on the walls of barn and sheds, or in one's place of business.
>
> The purpose of using the medal in any of the above ways is to call down God's blessing and protection upon us, wherever we are, and upon our homes and possessions, especially through the intercession of St. Benedict. By the conscious and devout use of the medal, it becomes, as it were, a constant silent prayer and reminder to us of our dignity as followers of Christ.
>
> **Origin of the Medal of Saint Benedict:** For the early Christians, the cross was a favorite symbol and badge of their faith in Christ. From the writings of St. Gregory the Great (540–604), we know that St. Benedict had a deep faith in the Cross and worked miracles with the sign of the cross. This faith in, and special devotion to the Cross was passed on to succeeding generations of Benedictines.
>
> Devotion to the Cross of Christ also gave rise to the striking of medals that bore the image of St. Benedict holding a cross aloft in his right hand and his Rule for Monasteries in the other hand. Thus, the Cross has always been closely associated with the Medal of St. Benedict, which is often referred to as the Medal-Cross of St. Benedict.

In the course of time, other additions were made, such as the Latin petition on the margin of the medal, asking that by St. Benedict's presence we may be strengthened in the hour of death, as will be explained later.

It is not known just when the first medal of St. Benedict was struck. At some point in history, a series of capital letters was placed around the large figure of the cross on the reverse side of the medal. For a long time, the meaning of these letters was unknown, but in 1647 a manuscript dating back to 1415 was found at the Abbey of Metten in Bavaria, giving an explanation of the letters. They are the initial letters of a Latin prayer of exorcism against Satan, as will be explained below.

**The Cross of Eternal Salvation:** On the face of the medal is the image of Saint Benedict. In his right hand he holds the cross, the Christian's symbol of salvation. The cross reminds us of the zealous work of evangelizing and civilizing England and Europe carried out mainly by the Benedictine monks and nuns, especially from the sixth to the ninth/tenth centuries.

**Rule and Raven:** In St. Benedict's left hand is his Rule for Monasteries that could well be summed up in the words of its Prologue, exhorting us to "walk in God's ways, with the Gospel as our guide." On a pedestal to the right of St. Benedict is the poisoned cup which shattered when he made the sign of the cross over it. On a pedestal to the left is a raven about to carry away a loaf of poisoned bread that a jealous enemy had sent to St. Benedict.

**C. S. P. B.:** Above the cup and the raven are the Latin words: *Crux s. patris Benedicti* (The Cross of our holy father Benedict). On the margin of the medal, encircling the figure of Benedict, are the Latin words: *Ejus in obitu nostro praesentia muniamur!* (May we be strengthened by his presence in the hour of our death!). Benedictines have always regarded St. Benedict as a special patron of a happy death. He himself died in the chapel at Montecasino while standing with his arms raised up to Heaven, supported by the brothers of the monastery, shortly after he received Holy Communion....

**Reverse Side of the Medal:** On the back of the medal, the cross is dominant. On the vertical and horizontal beams of the cross are the initial letters of a rhythmic Latin prayer: *Crux sancta sit mihi lux! Numquam draco sit mihi dux!* (May the holy cross be my light! May the dragon never be my guide!). In the angles of the cross, the letters *C S P B* stand for *Crux Sancti Patris Benedicti* (The cross of our holy father Benedict).

**Peace:** Above the cross is the word *pax* (peace) that has been a Benedictine motto for centuries. Around the margin of the back of the medal, the letters "V RS N S M V - S M Q L I V B" are the initial letters, as mentioned above, of a Latin prayer of exorcism against Satan: *Vade retro Satana! Numquam suade mihi vana! Sunt mala quae libas. Ipse venena bibas!* (Begone Satan! Never tempt me with your vanities! What you offer me is evil. Drink the poison yourself!)....

A profitable spiritual experience can be ours if we but take the time to study the array of inscriptions and representations found on the two sides of the medal. The lessons found there can be pondered over and over to bring true peace of mind and heart into our lives as we struggle to overcome the weaknesses of our human nature and realize that our human condition is not perfect, but that with the help of God and the intercession of the saints, our condition can become better. The Medal of St. Benedict can serve as a constant reminder of the need for us to take up our cross daily and "follow the true King, Christ our Lord," and thus learn "to share in his heavenly kingdom," as St. Benedict urges us in the Prologue of his Rule.[84]

*In my personal experience with this medal, which I do wear daily, I've seen some strange things happen. Multiple times, when people who are struggling with demonic possession or interference and perhaps are being treated by an exorcist have come up to me to ask me questions after one of my lectures, just the mere sight of my medal has caused them to start physically diabolically manifesting and to be in excruciating pain. Don't leave this powerful weapon sitting in the arsenal. Pick it up. Wear it. Use it in the fight.*

---

[84] "The Medal or Cross of St. Benedict," *Sisters of Carmel*, https://www.sistersofcarmel.com/about-the-st-benedict-medal/.

# Chapter 2

# Prayers Are Weapons Made of God's Words

*Our weapons are faith, prayer, and the sacraments:*
"For though we live in the world, we are not
carrying on a worldly war, for the weapons
of our warfare are not worldly but have
divine power to destroy strongholds."

— 2 Corinthians 10:3–4

*Prayer disperses evil spirits:* "The Lord also
thundered in the heavens, and the Most High
uttered his voice, hailstones and coals of fire.
And he sent out his arrows, and scattered them;
he flashed forth lightnings, and routed them."

— Psalm 18:13–14

*Arrows are a reference to the Word of God; because of
this, prayer is the same as calling in air strikes against
demons. In the Old Testament, in the middle of a battle,
the Israelites would position archers on top of the high
walls surrounding the city. When they would see an*

*enemy moving to attack the city, the archers would
launch volleys of arrows at the enemy, and the arrows
would fall upon them like rain:* "God shoots an arrow
at them; in a moment they are struck down."

— Psalm 64:8, NABRE

*When God speaks and chastens us, His Word
feels like arrows sinking into our body:* "O Lord,
rebuke me not in thy anger, nor chasten me
in thy wrath! For thy arrows have sunk into
me, and thy hand has come down on me."

—Psalm 38:1–2

*Alongside the idea of God's words as arrows, we can also think of certain prayers to Him as powerful arrows. An "arrow prayer" is a simple, short prayer that brings us right into the presence of God. These prayers are very often just a couple of words or a sentence. They can be short passages of Scripture, a cry for help, or just the Name of Jesus. As we think about our prayers as arrows, we should also keep in mind that the Greek word for sin in the New Testament is* hamartia, *which means, especially in terms of archery, "missing the mark." But when we shoot prayers like arrows to God, God gives us the grace to aiming straight in life and avoid sin.*

*Lions are a metaphor for the devil, but Scripture tells
us that God slays the lion-devils with His Word and
the military violence of the sword:* "My ravenous
enemies press upon me . . . like lions eager for
prey, like a young lion lurking in ambush. Rise,
O Lord, confront and cast them down; rescue

my soul from the wicked. Slay them with your
sword; with your hand, Lord, slay them."

> — Psalm 17:9, 12–14, NABRE

*Notice in these next two psalms how God sends forth
His Word throughout the cosmos through the angels:*
"The heavens are telling the glory of God.... Day to
day pours forth speech, and night to night declares
knowledge.... Yet their voice goes out through all
the earth, and their words to the end of the world."

> — Psalm 19:1–2, 4

"He sends his command to earth;
his word runs swiftly!

> — Psalm 147:15, NABRE

*The devil wants to give us death, but God wants
to give us life:* "I am very much afflicted, Lord;
give me life in accord with your word."

> — Psalm 119:107, NABRE

"Some fell sick from their wicked ways,
afflicted because of their sins.... In their
distress they cried to the Lord, who saved
them in their peril, sent forth his word to heal
them, and snatched them from the grave."

> — Psalm 107:17, 19–20, NABRE

*God's Word is called a rod, an offensive weapon.
God's word has an offensive nature to it:* "But he
shall judge the poor with justice, and decide

fairly for the land's afflicted. He shall strike the ruthless with the rod of his mouth, and with the breath of his lips he shall slay the wicked."

— Isaiah 11:4, NABRE

"And then the lawless one will be revealed, and the Lord Jesus will slay him with the breath of his mouth and destroy him by his appearing and his coming."

— 2 Thessalonians 2:8

*In Sacred Scripture, the sword is a reference to military violence. Although demons are spirits, they are pierced by the Word of God:* "For the word of God is living and active, sharper than any two-edged sword, piercing to the division of soul and spirit, of joints and marrow, and discerning the thoughts and intentions of the heart."

— Hebrews 4:12

"In his right hand he held seven stars. A sharp two-edged sword came out of his mouth, and his face shone like the sun at its brightest."

— Revelation 1:16, NABRE

"Therefore, repent. Otherwise, I will come to you quickly and wage war against them with the sword of my mouth."

— Revelation 2:16, NABRE

"The armies of heaven followed him, mounted on white horses and wearing clean white linen.

Out of his mouth came a sharp sword to strike the nations. He will rule them with an iron rod, and he himself will tread out in the wine press the wine of the fury and wrath of God the almighty. He has a name written on his cloak and on his thigh, 'King of kings and Lord of lords.'"

—Revelation 19:14–16, NABRE

*God's Word is so powerful it holds the universe together:* "He reflects the glory of God and bears the very stamp of his nature, upholding the universe by his word of power."

—Hebrews 1:3

*God's Word will speak truth to power and bring all wicked men to judgment:* "But by the same word the heavens and earth that now exist have been stored up for fire, being kept until the day of judgment and destruction of ungodly men."

—2 Peter 3:7

*In the next few verses, we see again that God's Word projects forth into the air and cosmos, affecting the spiritual realm. Our prayers come from our souls, and they are projected to the cosmos out of our mouths in vocal prayer and through our minds in meditative or contemplative prayer. And so our prayers are like a military airstrike against the demons in the air:* "By myself I have sworn, from my mouth has gone forth

in righteousness a word that shall not return: 'To me
every knee shall bow, every tongue shall swear.'"

—Isaiah 45:23

"So shall my word be that goes forth from my mouth;
It shall not return to me empty, but shall do what
pleases me, achieving the end for which I sent it."

—Isaiah 55:11, NABRE

"Then the Lord said to me: You have seen well,
for I am watching over my word to carry it out."

—Jeremiah 1:12, NABRE

"Therefore, thus says the Lord, the God of
hosts, because you have said this — See! I
make my words a fire in your mouth, and this
people the wood that it shall devour!"

—Jeremiah 5:14, NABRE

"Is not my word like fire, says the Lord, and like
a hammer which breaks the rock in pieces?"

—Jeremiah 23:29

"In all circumstances, hold faith as a shield, to
quench all [the] flaming arrows of the evil one.
And take the helmet of salvation and the sword
of the Spirit, which is the word of God."

—Ephesians 6:16–17, NABRE

*Prayer is like firing a winning shot:* "Prayer is the
first weapon ... for the ministers of the Church,
all those who have positions of responsibility."

— Fr. François-Marie Dermine[85]

*In the gift of the Holy Spirit, God the Father has
given us everything we need in order to live a holy
life, to be* "conformed to the image of his Son,"
*and so we possess the power to resist the devil:*
"God has sent forth the Spirit of his Son into
our hearts, crying out, 'Abba, Father!'"

— Romans 8:29, NABRE; Galatians 4:6, NABRE

[85] Solène Tadié, "Longtime Exorcist: Satanism Is Growing in Western Societies," *National Catholic Register*, December 4, 2020, https://www.
ncregister.com/interview/longtime-exorcist-satanism-is-growing-
in-western-societies.

# Chapter 3

# The Power and Reason of Spoken Words

As others have said *before me, demons are lawyers from Hell. They know the "spiritual laws" given by God, one which is that demons have a strong aversion to prayer. Prayer torments demons and drives them away: it repels them because of their very nature, and they cannot change their own nature.*

*We see the power of prayer at work when Our Lord prayed the Scriptures against Satan during His temptation, which is recorded in Matthew 4:1–11. Jesus' prayers torment the devil and drive him away. In the first temptation, Satan tells Jesus to make bread from stones since He is so hungry from fasting. Jesus replies, "It is written, 'Man shall not live by bread alone'" (Deut. 8:3); He fights against Satan's temptation with a prayer from Scripture. In the second temptation, Satan takes Jesus to the pinnacle of the temple and encourages Him to cast Himself down. Then, twisting the words of Scripture in an attempt to deceive Jesus Himself—using the words he hates for evil purpose—Satan boldly quotes Scripture, Psalm 91:11–12, telling Jesus that God would deliver Him. But Jesus responds, "You shall not tempt the Lord your God" (Deut. 6:16). In the third temptation, Satan takes Jesus up to a high mountain and shows Him all the kingdoms of the world, saying that he will give them to Him if He simply bows down to worship him. Jesus of course rejects this too, and He speaks an imprecatory prayer of rebuke and references Deuteronomy 6:13 when He says, "Begone, Satan! For it is written, 'You shall worship the Lord your God, and Him only shall you serve.'"*

*Satan was offering Jesus an "easy" path. It was also a selfish path, one that would leave us without hope, and of course Jesus recognized it for what it was. Matthew 4:11 concludes the story: "Then the devil left him, and behold, angels came and ministered to him." Notice that the spoken Word of God drove the devil away, and then angels came immediately. That's what happens when we pray: the devils are driven away, and angels come and encamp around us (see Psalm 34:7). Let us read now about the power of our words and the Word of God.*

"Words which do not give the light of
Christ increase the darkness."

— St. Teresa of Calcutta (1910–1997)

"I tell you, on the day of judgment people will
render an account for every careless word they
speak. By your words you will be acquitted,
and by your words you will be condemned."

— Matthew 12:36–37, NABRE

"In the same way the tongue is a small member and
yet has great pretensions. Consider how small a fire
can set a huge forest ablaze. The tongue is also a fire.
It exists among our members as a world of malice,
defiling the whole body and setting the entire course
of our lives on fire, itself set on fire by Gehenna.
For every kind of beast and bird, of reptile and sea
creature, can be tamed and has been tamed by the

human species, but no human being can tame the tongue. It is a restless evil, full of deadly poison."

—James 3:5–8, NABRE

"Let us hope!… [His] heart is so tender that he gives powers to his disciples for the good of humankind.… Let us therefore hope because of the Sacred Heart of Jesus!… God is so good that he orders his representatives, each time they enter a home, to utter these words: 'Peace to this home.' And he commits himself to make such words effective, bringing forth the peace they express, making it actually descend from Heaven on this home at the very moment the words are uttered, provided that the souls inhabiting it do not of themselves reject peace through ill will."

— Charles de Foucald (1858–1916), *Hope in the Gospels*

*Just as God gives us prayer and Scripture to use as arrows against the devil, the devil lets his own arrows fly back at us. What are the flaming arrows the devil uses to attack us? Just like us, he uses words. Americans like to say, "Sticks and stones may break my bones, but words will never hurt me," but this saying is not true here. Demons will use words against us, and so we have to use words to hurt them back. On a personal level, we have to watch our speech to make sure it is clean. Demons look for inconsistencies in speech and actions, since these inconsistencies represent vulnerabilities. Our true weapon is the Word of God, which is where all Catholic prayer comes from.*

"O God, hear my anguished voice; from a dreadful foe protect my life. Hide me from the malicious crowd, the mob of evildoers. They sharpen their tongues like swords, bend their bows of poison words. They shoot at the innocent from ambush, they shoot him in a moment and do not fear."

— Psalm 64:2–5, NABRE

"I call to God Most High, to God who provides for me. May God send help from Heaven to save me, shame those who trample upon me. May God send fidelity and mercy. I must lie down in the midst of lions hungry for human prey. Their teeth are spears and arrows; their tongue, a sharpened sword."

— Psalm 57:3–5, NABRE

"A murderous arrow is their tongue."

—Jeremiah 9:7, NABRE

*Demons are the terrors of night (see Job 4:12–16). They attack you in your dreams. This sort of attack, together with other things, can be called demonic obsession, which is mental distress caused by a demon. Demons keep a constantly running commentary inside the heads of the people they have possessed. But God promises to protect us so that* "You will not fear the terror of the night, nor the arrow that flies by day."

— Psalm 91:5

"The symptoms of diabolical obsession include sudden attacks at times ongoing, of obsessive thoughts (like pornography, violence, lust, hate, anger, blasphemy against what is holy) that the victim is unable to free himself of. Therefore, the obsessed person lives in a perpetual state of prostration, desperation, and attempts at suicide. Almost always obsession influences your dreams."

— Fr. Gabriele Amorth, *An Exorcist Tell His Story*

"O Jesus, I am locking myself in Your most merciful Heart as in a fortress, impregnable against the missiles of my enemies."

— St. Faustina Kowalska (1905–1938), *Diary*, no. 1535

*Demons use words as weapons of deception:* "But I am afraid that as the serpent deceived Eve by his cunning, your thoughts will be led astray from a sincere and pure devotion to Christ."

—2 Corinthians 11:3

*Eve's curiosity tempted her to the point of disobeying God and listening to the talking snake who was speaking lies:* "For Adam was formed first, then Eve; and Adam was not deceived, but the woman was deceived and became a transgressor."

—1 Timothy 2:13–14

# CHAPTER 4

# Angels and Demons Battle for Us

*The angels are here to help us:* "Are they not all
ministering spirits sent forth to serve, for the
sake of those who are to obtain salvation?"

— Hebrews 1:14

"For he will give his angels charge of
you to guard you in all your ways."

— Psalm 91:11

*But demons are always on the attack; you must
constantly resist them:* "Be sober, be watchful. Your
adversary the devil prowls around like a roaring lion,
seeking someone to devour. Resist him, firm in your
faith, knowing that the same experience of suffering is
required of your brotherhood throughout the world."

— 1 Peter 5:8–9

" 'God opposes the proud, but gives grace to the
humble.' Submit yourselves therefore to God.
Resist the devil and he will flee from you."

— James 4:6–7

*If you fail to put on the full armor of God, you will not be able to stand against the wiles and deceptions of the devil. Failure to recognize that we are at war (hence the term "Church Militant"), that we must fight the enemy with supernatural weapons, will result in an individual's eventual conformity to the world and the eventual loss of your soul:* "Do you not know that friendship with the world is enmity with God? Therefore whoever wishes to be a friend of the world makes himself an enemy of God."

—James 4:4

*It's that simple. There can be no compromise:* "For our struggle is not with flesh and blood but with the principalities, with the powers, with the world rulers of this present darkness, with the evil spirits in the heavens. Therefore, put on the armor of God, that you may be able to resist on the evil day and, having done everything, to hold your ground."

— Ephesians 6:12–13, NABRE

*This verse from Genesis describes the ordinary activity of a demon in its fight to gain influence over us, otherwise known as an "ordinary temptation":* "The Lord said to Cain, 'Why are you angry and why has your countenance fallen? If you do well, will you not be accepted? And if you do not do well, sin is crouching at the door; its desire is for you, but you must master it.'"

— Genesis 4:6–7

*Demons are opportunists; they wait and watch and are
ready to take advantage of any weakness that we show:
"Be angry but do not sin; do not let the sun go down
on your anger, and give no opportunity to the devil."*

— Ephesians 4:26–27

*The number one reason why people are afflicted
by demons is because they don't know their faith.
This is the biggest reason that people are weak,
and demons see opportunities to attack: "My
people are destroyed for lack of knowledge."*

— Hosea 4:6

*There is a popular story of a Bernardine sister who was once shown the
vast desolation of the devil throughout the world. As she saw his many
horrors and, she simultaneously heard the Blessed Virgin telling her that
Hell had been loosed upon the earth — now it was time to pray to her as
Queen of Angels and to ask the Heavenly Legions to engage in combat
against the forces of evil. The sister said to Mary, "But, my good Mother,
you who are so kind, could you not send them without our asking?" "No,"
Our Lady answered, "because prayer is one of the conditions required by
God Himself for obtaining favors." Then the Blessed Virgin communicated
the following prayer:*

August Queen of Heaven, sovereign Mistress of the Angels, who didst receive from the beginning the mission and the power to crush the serpent's head, we beseech thee to send thy holy angels, that under thy command and by thy power, they may pursue the evil spirits, encounter them on every side, resist their bold attacks, and drive them hence into the abyss of woe. Most holy Mother, send thy angels to defend us and to drive the cruel enemy from us. All ye holy angels and archangels, help and defend us. Amen. O good and tender Mother! Thou shalt ever be our Love and our Hope. Holy Angels and Archangels, keep and defend us. Amen.[86]

*May we keep this prayer in mind as we face the evils in the world each day, as we look to the angels to be our mediators and ask for their guidance and protection.*

> "Now when you, Tobit, and Sarah prayed,
> it was I who presented the record of your
> prayer before the Glory of the Lord.... I am
> Raphael, one of the seven angels who stand
> and serve before the Glory of the Lord."
>
> — Tobit 12:12, 15, NABRE

> "Now in Caesarea there was a man named Cornelius,
> a centurion of the Cohort called the Italica,
> devout and God-fearing along with his whole
> household, who used to give alms generously to
> the Jewish people and pray to God constantly.
> One afternoon about three o'clock, he saw plainly
> in a vision an angel of God come in to him and
> say to him, 'Cornelius.' He looked intently at him
> and, seized with fear, said, 'What is it, sir?' He
> said to him, 'Your prayers and almsgiving have
> ascended as a memorial offering before God.'"
>
> — Acts 10:1–4, NABRE

---

[86] "A Prayer to Our Lady, Queen of Angels, for Protection," *Tradition in Action*, https://mail.traditioninaction.org/religious/b006rp.htm.

*The movie The Greatest Miracle (2011) is an animated story about the unseen spiritual influences in our daily lives who are especially present when we attend and pray at Holy Mass. The movie even shows angels carrying our prayers to Heaven. One of the prayers of the priest within the Mass indicates this role of the angels:* "In humble prayer we ask you, almighty God: command that these gifts be borne by the hands of your holy angel to your altar on high in the sight of your divine majesty."

— Eucharist Prayer I of the Roman Canon

"Not only do angels present our supplications to the Lord, they also bestow upon us God's favor and blessings; guiding us, as good shepherds by way of their sweet communications and divine inspirations. Like the Good Shepherd, these heavenly friends protect us from prowling wolves, so says St. John of the Cross. As a result, if one desires to approach God unimpeded in his exercise of divine love, it is enough to have recourse to angels with a simple invocation. They are delighted to oblige since it is their God given mission."

— Fr. Cliff Ermatinger, *The Devil's Role in the Spiritual Life*

*In the story of Jacob's Ladder in the Old Testament, the ladder signifies the divine connection between God in Heaven and Jacob and his family on earth. Angels carry Jacob's prayers to Heaven and then carry God's grace back down to Jacob. The ladder reminded Jacob of the*

*presence of God's grace in his life and encouraged him
to fulfill the destiny of his people. After the revelations of
this dream, Jacob makes a vow: "If God will be with me
and protect me on this journey I am making and give
me food to eat and clothes to wear, and I come back
safely to my father's house, the Lord will be my God."*

— Genesis 28:20–21, NABRE

*Angels assist our prayers going upward to Heaven and help them to be
delivered as strategic airstrikes that injure demons. Some of the heavy hit-
ters in projecting these airstrikes are Catholic monasteries, which serve as
fortresses of prayer power and strategic forward operating bases in the
battles of spiritual warfare that rage between angels and demons for human
souls. In monasteries, men strive to live lives that are clean, ordered, and
have consistent prayer. This prayer is scheduled routinely at particular
times of each day in the Liturgy of the Hours. We too need this order and
ritual in order to strengthen our prayer lives and our arsenal for spiritual
battle. We will look in a later chapter at some additional quotations to
help us meditate on this need for order.*

# CHAPTER 5

# Demons Are in the Air — and We Fight Them in the Air

*As spiritual beings, demons work against us in
what we know as the air around us. Because of this,
Fr. Ripperger says that the ringing of an exorcised bell
can actually be a form of weaponizing against the
enemy. Indeed, the ringing of church bells, indoors
and outdoors, reminds demons of the Consecration at
Mass and reminds the angelic realm of the Incarnation.
Church bells are blessed, are consecrated for holy use,
and are powerful weapons against demonic activity.*
"By sounding the exorcized bell, in effect, the exorcism is
transmitted through the air and drives the demons out."

— Fr. Ripperger

*As we pray, we need to remember that our prayers also project into the air.
What does this mean? To project something means to throw it forward, or
to use your voice forcefully enough that you can be heard at distance — like
an image being projected onto the big screen in a theater. As you think
about using your voice in prayer, joining in the battle of the air and cosmos
around and above us, you should also remember two Greek words, aeros,*

*which means heavenly places, or of the air, and kosmos, which means order, form, arrangement, the world or universe. Keep these definitions in mind as you reflect on the next quotation.*

"When we pray, especially intoning the Name of Jesus and Mary, the words of our prayers flash across the sky, the cosmos, the eons, and the ages. The imagery is very difficult for a demon to hear. Projecting our prayer makes the image present to the demon. Angels and demons communicate through such projection, project thoughts into the cosmos. Joining with the angels, through our prayers, we should project sacred images into the cosmos; this is spiritual warfare. This is done through the mind. Our imagination brings forth a concept, and we will it out into the cosmos. Let me give you an analogy: demons project nightmares to your imagination. Think about the most horrible, scary, gruesome, macabre zombie monster figure appearing to you as you sleep. We call that a nightmare. You wake up hyperventilating, sweating, and you turn on the lights, looking around your room like a cornered, frightened mouse."

— Kyle Clement

"The devil whispered in my ear, 'You're not strong enough to withstand the storm.' Today I whispered in the devil's ear, 'I am a child of God, a man of faith, a warrior of Christ. I am the storm.'"

— Unknown

"And you he made alive, when you were dead through the trespasses and sins in which you once walked, following the course of this world, following the prince of the power of the air, the spirit that is now at work in the sons of disobedience. Among these we all once lived in the passions of our flesh, following the desires of body and mind, and so we were by nature children of wrath, like the rest of mankind."

— Ephesians 2:1–3

"And to make all men see what is the plan of the mystery hidden for ages in God who created all things; that through the church the manifold wisdom of God might now be made known to the principalities and powers in the heavenly places."

— Ephesians 3:9–10

*Catholic biblical tradition identifies locusts as demons; in this quotation from Revelation, we see them rise in the air like smoke and darken the sky:* "And the fifth angel blew his trumpet, and I saw a star fallen from heaven to earth, and he was given the key of the shaft of the bottomless pit; he opened the shaft of the bottomless pit, and from the shaft rose smoke like the smoke of a great furnace, and the sun and the air were darkened with the smoke from the shaft. Then from the smoke came locusts on the earth, and they were given power like the power of scorpions of the earth."

— Revelation 9:1–3

"It is a bigger miracle to be patient and
refrain from anger than it is to control the
demons which fly through the air."

— St. John Cassian, 360–435 A.D.

*Our prayer rises into the air like incense:* "Let my
prayer be counted as incense before thee; and the
lifting up of my hands as an evening sacrifice."

— Psalm 141:2

*God's Word is like the "stench of death" to those who
are going to Hell; think, then, how God's Word must
stink to the nostrils of a demon:* "St. Paul rejoices that
the gospel is being disseminated, like the fragrance
of incense, throughout the world as a result of his
ministry. It emits the sweet aroma of eternal life
to believers on the way to salvation and the stench
of death to those who are headed for spiritual
ruins. The terms fragrance and aroma are drawn
from [Old Testament] passages that describe the
pleasing odor of sacrifices offered to the Lord (see
Gen. 8:21; Exod. 29:18; Lev. 1:9; Num. 15:3)."

— Dr. Scott Hahn

"But thanks be to God, who always leads us in
triumph in Christ and manifests through us the odor
of the knowledge of him in every place. For we are
the aroma of Christ for God among those who are
being saved and among those who are perishing."

— 2 Corinthians 2:14–15, NABRE

*When we pray, we know that the saints are with us; we
are "surrounded by so great a cloud of witnesses."*

— Hebrews 12:1

*Our prayer is lifted through the air by the ministry
of angels:* "The smoke of the incense along
with the prayers of the holy ones went up
before God from the hand of the angel."

— Revelation 8:4, NABRE

"The incense symbolizes our prayer."

— *The Roman Catholic Daily Missal*[87]

87   *The Roman Catholic Daily Missal* (Dickenson, TX: Angelus Press, 1962),
865.

# CHAPTER 6

# Faith, Cleanliness, and Order

*IF YOU ARE IN a state of grace, in a right relationship with God, your prayers are a clean and unblemished offering to God, ascending like incense to Heaven just like the prayers of the righteous Abel. In this state of grace, this state of holiness, you are best able to receive the gift of spiritual discernment. You are best able to distinguish, or discern, between the clean and the unclean. On the other side of the coin, we see Abel's brother, Cain, referenced twice in the New Testament as an unrighteous person (1 John 3:12; Jude 1:11). His sacrifice was not acceptable to God because the state of his soul was not acceptable to God. If you are in this state of uncleanness, demons will be more attracted to you — like attracts like, and unclean spirits are attracted to unclean people. In the New Testament, demons that possess people are referred to as "unclean spirits" twenty-one times; we also see the connection between uncleanliness and evil when our Lord casts the legion of demons into a herd of pigs (Matt. 8:28–34; Mark 5:1–20; Luke 8:26–39); as pigs were considered unclean under Jewish law (see Lev. 11:7). What does this idea mean for us? To put it bluntly, if you live in mortal sin, then your soul is unclean, and you are a target: you look like a spiritual pig to the demons, and they will be attracted to you.*

"We know that God does not listen to
sinners, but if anyone is a worshiper of God
and does his will, God listens to him."

—John 9:31

*What is "the will of God?" For you to be saved
(1 Tim. 2:3–4) and for you to become holy and shun
immorality (1 Thes. 4:3; 2 Tim. 1:9). God wants you
to repent and turn away from your sin:* "If my people
who are called by my name humble themselves,
and pray and seek my face, and turn from their
wicked ways, then I will hear from heaven, and
will forgive their sin and heal their land."

—2 Chronicles 7:14

*Scripture teaches us that we must be able to know the
difference between what is clean and what is unclean,
what is good and what is sin, so that we may walk in
the way of God. Although these verses were spoken
as a particular dictate for the Levites in the Old
Testament, the final principle is applicable to all of
our lives:* "The Lord said to Aaron: When you are
to go to the tent of meeting, you and your sons
are forbidden, by a perpetual statute throughout
your generations, to drink any wine or strong
drink, lest you die. You must be able to distinguish
between what is sacred and what is profane, and
between what is clean and what is unclean."

—Leviticus 10:8–10, NABRE

*This next admonition to "be sober," if taken to heart, would save many people from a tragic end. How many hundreds of thousands have died in the drug crisis? How many DUIs have resulted in untimely deaths? Scripture warns us:* "Be sober, be watchful. Your adversary the devil prowls around like a roaring lion, seeking someone to devour. Resist him, firm in your faith."

— 1 Peter 5:8–9

*Indeed, we must be vigilant, for our adversary has nothing less than lethal intentions:* "Let your heart hold fast my words; keep my commandments, and live."

— Proverbs 4:4

*And we must keep our faith:* "But without faith it is impossible to please him, for anyone who approaches God must believe that he exists and that he rewards those who seek him."

— Hebrews 11:6, NABRE

*To be faithful requires internal order and discipline. These are the attributes of a soldier prepared for battle. Faithlessness, however, suggests someone who is unreliable, inconsistent, deceptive, or guilty of betrayal. These attributes can be easily observed in Judas Iscariot, whose faithlessness opened him up to the diabolical and led him to do the unthinkable in the betrayal of our Lord:* "Jesus said to him, 'He who has bathed does not need to wash, except for his feet, but he is clean all over; and you are clean,

but not all of you.' For he knew who was to betray
him; that was why he said, 'You are not all clean.'"

—John 13:10–11

"But as for the cowardly, the faithless, the polluted,
as for murderers, fornicators, sorcerers, idolaters,
and all liars, their lot shall be in the lake that burns
with fire and brimstone, which is the second death."

—Revelation 21:8

"Blessed are the clean of heart, for they will see God."

—Matthew 5:8, NABRE

"When Jesus came down from the mountain, great
crowds followed him. And then a leper approached,
did him homage, and said, 'Lord, if you wish, you
can make me clean.' He stretched out his hand,
touched him, and said, 'I will do it. Be made
clean.' His leprosy was cleansed immediately."

—Matthew 8:1–3, NABRE

"Who may go up the mountain of the Lord?
Who can stand in his holy place? 'The clean
of hand and pure of heart, who has not given
his soul to useless things, what is vain.'"

—Psalm 24:3–4, NABRE

"A clean heart create for me, God; renew
within me a steadfast spirit."

—Psalm 51:12, NABRE

"For God has not called us for
uncleanness, but in holiness."

— 1 Thessalonians 4:7

*Scripture and the great thinkers of our Church have taken this idea of faith and faithlessness, cleanliness and uncleanliness, one step further. What leads to the virtues of faith and spiritual cleanliness? Quite simply, it is order, stemming from a discipline that recognizes who we are in God's creation and what our relationship is with the people and the rest of the world around us. As Kyle Clement once said to me:* "Men need fraternity, order, and ritual to combat the diabolical."

*Scripture, too, speaks of fraternity:* "Iron sharpens
iron, and one man sharpens another."

— Proverbs 27:17

*Regarding our need for order, the Bible teaches:* "For
though I am absent in body, yet I am with you in
spirit, rejoicing to see your good order and the
firmness of your faith in Christ. As therefore you
received Christ Jesus the Lord, so live in him, rooted
and built up in him and established in the faith, just
as you were taught, abounding in thanksgiving."

— Colossians 2:5–7

*And regarding our need for ritual, the Bible says:*
"Therefore King Darius signed the document and
interdict. When Daniel knew that the document
had been signed, he went to his house where he
had windows in his upper chamber open toward
Jerusalem; and he got down upon his knees three

times a day and prayed and gave thanks before his God, as he had done previously. Then these men came by agreement and found Daniel making petition and supplication before his God."

—Daniel 6:9–11

"He is not the God of disorder but of peace."

—1 Corinthians 14:33, NABRE

"For where jealousy and selfish ambition exist, there is disorder and every foul practice."

—James 3:16, NABRE

"For I fear that when I come I may find you not such as I wish, and that you may find me not as you wish; that there may be rivalry, jealousy, fury, selfishness, slander, gossip, conceit, and disorder."

—2 Corinthians 12:20, NABRE

"But everything must be done properly and in order."

—1 Corinthians 14:40, NABRE

"For this cause I left thee in Crete, that thou shouldest set in order the things that are wanting, and shouldest ordain priests in every city, as I also appointed thee."

—Titus 1:5, Douay-Rheims

"For even if I am absent in the flesh, yet I am with you in spirit, rejoicing as I observe your good order and the firmness of your faith in Christ."

—Colossians 2:5, NABRE

*Our God is a God of order: just look at the first two chapters of Genesis. Out of chaos, God brings perfect order and harmony:* " 'The earth was without form and void.' In the original Hebrew, *tohu wabohu* are the two words which describe primordial earth's twofold condition: formlessness and emptiness. God transforms earth from chaos to cosmos according to his power and plan."

— Scott Hahn, *A Father Who Keeps His Promises*

"The demons are scared to death of all good, holy, rightly ordered families."

— Fr. Ripperger, private correspondence

"Disorder in society is the result of disorder in the family."

— St. Angela Merici (1474–1540)

"Catholicism is the law of life, the life of the intelligence, the solution of all problems. Catholicism is the truth, and everything that departs from it one iota is disorder, deception, and error."

—Juan Donoso Cortes (1809–1853), *Essays on Catholicism, Liberalism, and Socialism*

# Chapter 7

# The Saints and Catholic Writers on Prayer

"A saint is someone who is solidly pious, someone deeply convinced that prayer is as necessary for his soul as food is for his body; someone for whom prayer is a necessity and a consolation, and who consequently remains steadfast in his exercises of piety and who neglects nothing in order to perform them as best as he can."

— St. Marcellin Champagnat (1789–1840)[88]

"Prayer is conversation with God."

— Attributed to St. Clement of Alexandria (150–215 A.D.)

"Father, there will be nothing difficult here, provided we have a crucifix.... The word of the Lord is a light for the mind and a fire for the will, so that man may know and love God.... It is a weapon against a heart

---

[88] Quoted in "The Food of Sanctity, the Food of Eternal Life" in *Magnificat* 25, no. 1 (April 2023), 314.

stubbornly entrenched in vice. It is a sword against the flesh, the world and the devil to destroy every sin."

— St. Lawrence of Brindisi (1559–1619)[89]

"Our Lady appeared to him, accompanied by three angels, and she said, 'Dear Dominic, do you know which weapon the Blessed Trinity wants to use to reform the world?' 'Oh, my Lady,' answered St. Dominic, 'you know far better than I do, because next to your Son Jesus Christ you have always been the chief instrument of our salvation.' Then our Lady replied, 'I want you to know that, in this kind of warfare, the principal weapon has always been the Angelic Psalter, which is the foundation-stone of the New Testament. Therefore, if you want to reach these hardened souls and win them over to God, preach my Psalter.'"

— St. Louis-Marie de Montfort (1673–1716)[90]

"Prayer is the best weapon we possess, the key that opens the heart of God."

— St. Padre Pio (1887–1968)

"However great may be the temptation, if we know how to use the weapon of prayer well, we shall come off as conquerors at last, for prayer is more powerful than all the demons. He who is attacked by the spirits

[89]   Quoted in "Meditation of the Day" in *Magnificat* 22, no. 5 (July 2020), 301.
[90]   St. Louis-Marie de Montfort, *Secret of the Rosary*, quoted in "St. Dominic Receives the Rosary," *Dominican Friars Foundation*, https://dominican-friars.org/st-dominic-receiving-rosary/.

of darkness needs only to apply himself vigorously to
prayer, and he will beat them back with great success."

— St. Bernard of Clairvaux (1090–1153)

"I have already told you that I hold you in My
hands as an arrow. I now want you to hurl this
arrow against My enemies. To arm you for battle
ahead, I give you the weapons of My Passion,
that is My Cross which these enemies dread, and
also the other instruments of My tortures."

—Jesus to Sr. Mary of St. Peter (1816–1848),
as recorded in her autobiography, *The Golden
Arrow: The Revelations of Sr. Mary of St. Peter*

"Prayer, without a doubt, is the most powerful
weapon the Lord gives us to conquer evil … but
we must really put ourselves into prayer. It is not
enough just to say the words; it must come from the
heart. And also prayer needs to be continuous.…
The warfare in which we are engaged is ongoing,
so our prayer must be ongoing as well."

— St. Alphonsus Liguori (1696–1787)

"They [demons] have no power except against
cowardly souls who surrender their weapons."

— St. Teresa of Ávila (1515–1582)

"Whenever my enemy provokes me to
combat, I try to behave like a soldier."

— St. Thérèse of Lisieux (1873–1897)

"Christians are born for combat."

— Pope Leo XIII (1810–1903)

"Do not be despondent when fighting against
the incorporeal enemy, but even in the midst of
your afflictions and oppression, praise the Lord,
who has found you worthy to suffer for Him, by
struggling against the subtlety of the serpent,
and to be wounded for Him at every hour;
for had you not lived piously, and endeavored
to become united to God, the enemy would
not have attacked and tormented you."

— John of Kronstadt (1829–1909)

# Chapter 8

# The Role of Prayer in the Power of Redemptive Suffering

*We can all recognize certain situations or experiences in our life as unfortunate, painful, or even unjust. And we all have particular faults and weaknesses that may, to some extent, be caused by psychological factors, family history, or other factors beyond our control. But just having been dealt a difficult hand, either in general or in particular ways, doesn't negate that old childish saying that two wrongs don't make a right. Even and especially in difficult times and in tough circumstances, we are called — with our unique deficiencies, struggles, and crosses — to unite ourselves to Christ and to seek to grow in virtue. We can't start acting badly because we've been dealt a bad hand. And, in fact, it is because of our crosses and weaknesses that we're able to suffer more, be joined more closely to Christ, and so be more capable of helping to redeem the world through suffering.*

*In this first quotation, St. Paul is silent on what the "thorn" refers to, although he makes it clear that he wishes that, whatever it was, he didn't have to deal with it. But the Lord allowed Paul to suffer so he would realize his dependence on God. The "thorn" was obviously unpleasant, but it was part of Paul's road to perfection in Christ: "And to keep me from being* too elated by the abundance of revelations, a thorn was given me in the flesh, a messenger of Satan, to harass me, to keep me from being too elated. Three times I besought the Lord about this, that it should leave me; but he said to me, 'My grace is sufficient for you, for my power is made perfect in weakness.' I will all the more gladly boast of my weaknesses, that the power of Christ may rest upon me."

— 2 Corinthians 12:7–9

*God will allow a person, especially the patriarch or matriarch of a family, to suffer for his family until enough grace has been mined out and merited through suffering for the offspring:* "Our interior disposition, our willingness to pray and suffer, are the marks of men. Our sufferings united to God is efficacious for other people in the mystical body of Christ. Being a follower of Christ is not a spectator sport. It requires your full participation."

— Kyle Clement, podcast interview on *Liber Christo War College Situation Room*

"The 'demonic matrix,' or 'demonic paradigm,' or 'demonic ideology' leads a person to habitual sin, a life of mortal sin, the elevation of self-pride. The demonic matrix is a set of rules: this is how the demon interacts with reality. Demons have a matrix-like coding, and they follow their fallen nature. The demonic matrix is psychological thought, how one plugs into reality. What militates against that, is when you offer up your sufferings. [Col. 1:24: 'Now

I rejoice in my sufferings for your sake, and in my flesh I complete what is lacking in Christ's afflictions for the sake of his body, that is, the church.'] It's not understandable to them. Demons say: 'Why would someone suffer for someone else's benefit? That does not compute.' When we force the demon to become the instrument of our sanctification or the salvation of others, it doesn't compute to them. This is a logic they cannot understand, and they will flee. They don't want to cooperate with making someone holy. Remember, they follow Satan who said, '*Non serviam*.' Pursuing holiness and avoiding vice breaks the demonic matrix."

— Dr. Dan Schneider, podcast interview on
*Liber Christo War College Situation Room*


"Job was turned over to the devil to be tempted so that, by withstanding the test, Job would become a torment to the devil."

— St. Augustine (354–440 A.D.)


*"Lukewarm" Catholicism seems to forget that God redeems suffering — and that our victory comes from the Cross. The following two verses, one from Proverbs and one from the First Letter of St. Peter, are linked in this idea:* "The crucible is for silver, and the furnace is for gold, and the Lord tries hearts"; "so that the genuineness of your faith, more precious than gold which though perishable

is tested by fire, may redound to praise and glory
and honor at the revelation of Jesus Christ."

— Proverbs 17:3, 1 Peter 1:7

"But the souls of the righteous are in the hand of
God, and no torment will ever touch them. In the
eyes of the foolish they seemed to have died, and
their departure was thought to be an affliction, and
their going from us to be their destruction; but they
are at peace. For though in the sight of men they
were punished, their hope is full of immortality.
Having been disciplined a little, they will receive
great good, because God tested them and found
them worthy of himself; like gold in the furnace
he tried them, and like a sacrificial burnt offering
he accepted them. . . . Those who trust in him will
understand truth, and the faithful will abide with
him in love, because grace and mercy are upon
his elect, and he watches over his holy ones."

— Wisdom 3:1–6, 9

"Those who suffer in accord with God's will hand
their souls over to a faithful creator as they do good."

— 1 Peter 4:19, NABRE

"If one member suffers, all suffer together; if one
member is honored, all rejoice together. Now you are
the body of Christ and individually members of it."

— 1 Corinthians 12:26–27

*As followers of Christ, through our own suffering,
we share in his suffering and death, which is the very
fountain of life for the world. Our sufferings and wounds
pour forth the love and power of Jesus Christ that
saves the world:* "We are afflicted in every way, but
not crushed; perplexed, but not driven to despair;
persecuted, but not forsaken; struck down, but
not destroyed; always carrying in the body the
death of Jesus, so that the life of Jesus may also be
manifested in our bodies. For while we live we are
always being given up to death for Jesus' sake, so
that the life of Jesus may be manifested in our mortal
flesh. So death is at work in us, but life in you."

— 2 Corinthians 4:8–12

*Christ's sufferings overflow to us, and the grace
merited from our sufferings overflows to others in
the mystical body of Christ, for we are all connected
through Christ, our head. That alone not only makes
sense out of our sufferings, but it turns them into
something with redemptive power. No religion other
than Christianity has really grasped that suffering can
be redemptive:* "For as Christ's sufferings overflow
to us, so through Christ does our encouragement
also overflow. If we are afflicted, it is for your
encouragement and salvation; if we are encouraged,
it is for your encouragement, which enables you
to endure the same sufferings that we suffer."

— 2 Corinthians 1:5–6, NABRE

"Now I rejoice in my sufferings for your sake, and in my flesh I complete what is lacking in Christ's afflictions for the sake of his body, that is, the church."

— Colossians 1:24

" 'What is lacking,' i.e., the suffering that remains for believers in the trials of life. Suffering is a mission for all of the faithful as a means of conforming ourselves to Christ (Rom. 8:17; Phil. 3:10). These words could be misunderstood to mean that the suffering of Christ was not sufficient for redemption and that the suffering of the saints must be added to complete it. This, however, would be heretical. Christ and the Church are one mystical person, and while the merits of Christ are infinite, the saints acquire merit in a limited degree. What is 'lacking,' then pertains to the afflictions of the entire Church, to which Paul adds his own amount."

— Dr. Scott Hahn, Ignatius Catholic Study Bible

"Suffering should be an imitation of God who took suffering upon Himself in this life. Our pain is a completion of what is lacking, as St. Paul says, in the sufferings of Christ. It makes the application of the merits of His Passion more effective. More souls can be saved as a result of our sufferings if they are united with those of Christ…. If you offer your sufferings for souls, you can save them better than a healthy person can. You see, Jesus Christ preached and performed many miracles, but only

a few people were converted. When He suffered
and died, though, He redeemed the whole world."

— Fr. Narciso Irala, S.J., "Practical
Remedies for Sadness."[91]

*Suffering is of such inestimable redemptive worth that
nothing equals it in Heaven or on earth:* "Suffering
in and of itself, separated from a supernatural
perspective, has no real value. If you like, suffering
either makes us *better or bitter.* In the Diary of St.
Faustina, the angels view the human person with
a holy envy and for two reasons. First, the human
person is capable of receiving the incredible Gift of
the most Holy Eucharist — the Body, Blood, Soul,
and Divinity of Jesus in Holy Communion. The
angels in Heaven will never have this extraordinary
privilege. Also, the angels cannot suffer. The angels
understand that suffering, if viewed and accepted
properly, has infinite value and can be most pleasing
to God. In fact, Jesus, the Incarnate Word, chose the
path of suffering as the means by which the salvation
of the world would be consummated.... Nobody in
the world can avoid the reality of suffering. These
three short words sum up the entire message:
Offer it up! When God, in His infinite Wisdom,
decides to visit you with some form of suffering, it
is of enormous importance to accept the suffering
given from the loving and providential Hands of

[91] Fr. Narciso Irala, S.J., "Practical Remedies for Sadness," *Catholic Exchange,*
April 29, 2022, https://catholicexchange.com/practical-remedies-
for-sadness/.

God and offer it up. Remember, suffering can either make us *better* or *bitter*. Suffering can either save souls or be wasted! When we are suffering, let us strive to unite our suffering to the Cross — to the Passion, Death, and Resurrection of Jesus. This is sometimes called the Paschal Mystery of Christ. United with Jesus in our lives, actions, and especially our sufferings, there is infinite value.… Remember the short maxim: 'Suffering either makes you better or bitter.' Bitter, if one suffers for the mere sake of suffering! Better, sanctified and growing in holiness, only when our suffering is united with the suffering of Jesus on the Cross in Holy Mass."

— Fr. Edward Broom, O.M.V., "Learning to Offer Up Our Sacrifices and Sufferings"[92]

*We all have problems we can offer up. For the elderly among us, for example, there are almost always medical problems we experience as a form of suffering. But so long as you intentionally say a Morning Offering every day (there is one included in the prayers at the end of this book), every ache and pain is being offered to God as penance. It was St. Maximilian Kolbe who said that there are three stages of life: formation, or childhood; apostolate, or the filling out of your primary vocation in life; and suffering, which is the sickness of old age.*

---

[92]  Fr. Edward Broom, O.M.V., "Learning to Offer Up Our Sacrifices and Sufferings," *Fr. Ed Broom, OMV Oblates of the Virgin Mary*, January 31, 2021, http://fatherbroom.com/blog/2021/01/learning-to-offer-up-our-sacrifices-sufferings/.

*No matter what stage you are in now, you will meet suffering, and so you will meet a way to offer it up.*

*Edith Stein, who took the name Sr. Teresa Benedicta of the Cross as a Carmelite nun, was a Jewish-born German philosopher and a convert to Catholicism. Just like St. Maximilian Kolbe, she was martyred in Auschwitz. She said,* "Voluntary expiatory suffering is what truly and really unites one to the Lord intimately.... Only in union with the divine head does human suffering take on expiatory power."

— St. Teresa Benedicta of the
Cross (1891–1942)[93]

*When St. Thérèse of Lisieux was only fourteen years old, she offered prayers of reparation and personal suffering for the conversion of a death row convict who had killed two women and a child. Through her offerings, he repented at the last minute, just like the good thief, St. Dismas:* "In order still further to enkindle my ardor, Our Divine Master soon proved to me how pleasing to him was my desire. Just then I heard much talk of a notorious criminal, Pranzini, who was sentenced to death for several shocking murders, and, as he was quite impenitent, everyone feared he would be eternally lost. How I longed to avert this irreparable calamity! In order to do so I employed all the spiritual means I could

---

[93] Quoted in "Meditation of the Day," in *Magnificat* 23, no. 6 (August 2021), 125.

think of, and, knowing that my own efforts were unavailing, I offered for his pardon the infinite merits of Our Savior and the treasures of Holy Church.

"Need I say that in the depths of my heart I felt certain my request would be granted? But, that I might gain courage to persevere in the quest for souls, I said in all simplicity: 'My God, I am quite sure that Thou wilt pardon this unhappy Pranzini. I should still think so if he did not confess his sins or give any sign of sorrow, because I have such confidence in Thy unbounded Mercy; but this is my first sinner, and therefore I beg for just one sign of repentance to reassure me.' My prayer was granted to the letter. My Father never allowed us to read the papers, but I did not think there was any disobedience in looking at the part about Pranzini. The day after his execution I hastily opened the paper, *La Croix*, and what did I see? Tears betrayed my emotion; I was obliged to run out of the room. Pranzini had mounted the scaffold without confessing or receiving absolution, and the executioners were already dragging him towards the fatal block, when all at once, apparently in answer to a sudden inspiration, he turned round, seized the crucifix which the priest was offering to him, and kissed Our Lord's Sacred Wounds three times."

St. Thérèse of Lisieux (1873–1897)[94]

94   St. Thérèse of Lisieux, *The Story of a Soul*, trans. Thomas N. Taylor (London: Burns, Oates, and Washbourne, 1922); available at *Project Gutenberg*, https://www.gutenberg.org/cache/epub/16772/pg16772-images.html.

*Through our suffering, we distribute graces to other people in the Body of Christ. This is why, when Our Lady appeared to the children of Fatima she said:* "Pray, pray a great deal, and make sacrifices for sinners, for many souls go to Hell, because they have no one to pray and make sacrifices for them."

The Blessed Virgin Mary at
Fatima, August 19, 1917

"The Gospel of suffering is being written unceasingly, and it speaks unceasingly with the words of this strange paradox: the springs of divine power gush forth precisely in the midst of human weakness. Those who share in the sufferings of Christ preserve in their own sufferings a very special particle of the infinite treasure of the world's Redemption and can share this treasure with others."

Pope St. John Paul II, apostolic
letter *Salvifici Doloris*, no. 27

*Fr. Gabriel of St. Mary Magdalen was a Discalced Carmelite priest, confessor, and spiritual director. Most likely a mystic himself, he was also an expert in the writings of such venerated Carmelite Mystics as St. Teresa of Ávila and St. John of the Cross. He writes in his book of daily meditations,* Divine Intimacy: "We can never be certain at all that our prayers will be answered according to our expectation, for we do not know if what we ask is conformable to God's will; but when it is a question of apostolic prayer which asks for grace and the salvation of souls, it is a very different matter. In fact, when we pray for the aims of the apostolate, we are fitting into the plan prearranged by God Himself from all eternity, that plan for the salvation of all men which God desires to put into action infinitely more than we do; therefore, we cannot doubt the efficacy of our prayer. Because of this effectiveness, apostolic prayer is one of the most powerful means of furthering the apostolate."

Fr. Gabriel of St. Mary Magdalen,
O.C.D. (1893–1953)[95]

*Servant of God Fr. John A. Hardon spoke on the necessity of suffering in order to merit grace. He said that pain, especially the pain of the Cross, was the method of earning that grace.* "As St. Ignatius made clear, the heart of the apostolate is to be a channel of grace to others. Those who have the true faith are used by Christ to bring this faith to others. Patient people are instruments of grace to bring patience to those whose lives they touch. People who are humble communicate humility. Chaste Christians are conduits of chastity.... We read in St. Paul that he tells the Corinthians, 'In Christ Jesus, by the gospel, I have begotten you' (1 Cor. 4:15). There is

---

[95] As quoted in Michael Warren Davis, "Cardinal Robert Sarah's Guide to the New Counter-Reformation," *Crisis Magazine,* November 4, 2019, https://crisismagazine.com/opinion/cardinal-sarahs-guide-to-the-new-counter-reformation.

such a thing as fruitfulness of spirit. We not only can, we are obliged to reproduce ourselves spiritually."

Servant of God Fr. John A. Hardon, S.J.,
"*Evangelium Vitae*: Spiritual Combat
with the Culture of Death."[96]

*The following verse perfectly describes the distribution of graces, that is, how it is that what one person in the Body of Christ does well positively affects the other members of that Body. The good caused by the suffering that you offer to God in this life will be revealed to you in Heaven. God will show you the people you ended up blessing, saving, converting, healing from illness, and delivering from demons as a result of the suffering that you offered up. Your sufferings merit grace that God redistributes to the souls who need it:* "In the days of his flesh, Jesus offered up prayers and supplications, with loud cries and tears, to him who was able to save him from death, and he was heard for his godly fear. Although he was a Son, he learned obedience through what he suffered; and being made perfect he became the source of eternal salvation to all who obey him."

Hebrews 5:7–9

"Redemptive suffering takes us beyond our trials. The cruel reality of our situation is allowing evil to reach a climax. If we are to survive, we cannot face this danger alone. We must have recourse to

---

[96] Fr. John A. Hardon, S.J., "*Evangelium Vitae*: Spiritual Combat with the Culture of Death," *The Real Presence Association*, https://www.therealpresence.org/archives/Evangelization/Evangelization_008.htm.

the Church that teaches us how to overcome our
fears and embrace suffering. When united with
the infinitely precious suffering of Our Lord Jesus
Christ, we can share in His redemptive suffering.
We can offer up our sufferings for the salvation
of souls. Our sufferings then gain meaning and
purpose. They impact society and history. Thus, the
Christian perspective on suffering goes far beyond
our trials. It puts them in the context of eternity,
which should fill us with joy. Then we can truly say,
*"forsan et haec olim meminisse iuvabit"* ["and perhaps
it will please us one day to remember these things"
(Virgil, *Aeneid* 1.203)]. However, the joy will not
only be an earthly joy but also a heavenly one."

John Horvat II, "Virgil's 'Aeneid'
and the Value of Suffering"[97]

"Therefore, starting today, call to mind the sufferings
of your life. Place these precious jewels in the hands
and Heart of Mary. She will deposit them on the altar
of the Cross of Calvary. Your suffering united to Jesus
and Mary's suffering will indeed have infinite value
for the salvation of souls in time and for all eternity!"

Fr. Edward Broom, O.M.V., "Learning to
Offer Up Our Sacrifices and Sufferings"

"Servant of God Elizabeth Leseur has been called
the Thérèse of Lisieux for married women. And

---

[97]  John Horvat II, "Virgil's 'Aeneid' and the Value of Suffering," *The Imagi-
native Conservative,* April 13, 2021, https://theimaginativeconservative.
org/2021/04/virgil-aeneid-value-suffering-john-horvat.html.

she did, in fact, discover her own little way of
sanctification through pure and sacrificial love,
humility, meekness, redemptive suffering, a vibrant
prayer life, and, critically, shutting the heck up....

"In 1889 she married Felix Leseur, a medical
doctor from a similarly affluent background, but
no longer Catholic (a point she discovered only
shortly before their wedding). He not only refused
to practice Catholicism, he was outwardly and
vehemently hostile toward the faith, becoming
well-known as the editor of an atheistic and
anti-clerical Parisian newspaper at a time when
these opinions were the height of chic in Parisian
society. They entertained often and the guests
were invariably his atheistic friends. So forcefully
did he browbeat Elisabeth about Catholicism that
she (who was not then well-versed in Catholic
teaching) fell away from the Church for two years.

"At age thirty-two, however, she resumed practicing
her faith and began to read great spiritual works
to better defend it. With the aid of her spiritual
director, she began a disciplined program of life
grounded in her relationship with God. She had
always quietly performed charitable works — to the
extent her health allowed — and now, meditating
on the doctrine of the communion of saints,
her mission included offering her physical and
emotional suffering (which included the sorrow
of infertility), as well as her sacrifices and prayers

for the conversion and salvation of her husband,
relatives, friends, and for the souls in Purgatory.

"While actively engaged with the world and
the arrogant, atheistic Parisian society (where,
according to her husband, even the atheists
were attracted to her grace and holiness),
she simultaneously and unassumingly lived a
hidden life as a contemplative and mystic.

"Elisabeth's death in 1914, from breast cancer
that had metastasized, was prolonged and painful,
but Felix testified that she bore it with calm and
sweetness. She had asked her sister to destroy her
spiritual "Diary" after her death, but instead, her
sister gave it to Felix, who published it a few years
later. He was so moved by the profound faith and
love of his wife, that within a year, he returned to
Confession and the faith. Several years later, he
entered the Order of Preachers. Ordained nine
years after her death, Fr. Leseur spent much of his
time until his own death in 1950 speaking about her
spirituality and promoting her cause for sainthood."

Susan E. Wills, "Divorce-Proof Your Marriage by
Emulating Servant of God Elisabeth Leseur"[98]

---

[98] Susan E. Wills, "Divorce-Proof Your Marriage by Emulating Servant
of God Elisabeth Leseur," *Aleteia*, October 4, 2014, https://aleteia.
org/2014/10/04/divorce-proof-your-marriage-by-emulating-servant-
of-god-elisabeth-leseur.

*Here is another powerful story on redemptive suffering offered for others:* "Shortly before the reign of terror ended during the French Revolution, sixteen women offered their lives to God as a sacrifice on behalf of their country and countrymen. These women were all members of a Carmelite community which had been forced out of their convent two years earlier. Despite the persecution, they continued in common prayer, living out their vocations as best they could. In June of 1794, they were arrested and charged with 'conspiracy, treason, being royalists, and corresponding with anti-revolutionaries,' as well as 'attachment to your Religion and the King.' Tried by the kangaroo court of the New Republic, the evidence against them included their possession of a tablecloth embroidered with Sacred Heart Images; and the canticle of the Sacred Heart, a hymn of that time written by a Parisian Priest. Without defense, the nuns were condemned to death. They went to the guillotine, as one witness describes it, as though they were going to a wedding. And they sang as they went: the *Salva Regina, Te Deum, Veni Sancte Spiritus,* and *Laudate Dominum, Omnes Gentes.* Ten days after their death, the Reign of Terror came to its end with the arrest and execution of Robespierre. St. Pius X beatified these courageous women in 1906."

Rev. Sebastian White, "Saints Who Were Musicians"[99]

---

[99] Quoted in "Saints Who Were Musicians" in *Magnificat* 24, no. 2 (Holy Week 2022), 84.

"The foundation of fruitless suffering is the lack of friendship with Jesus, just as the foundation of fruitful suffering is union with Him. We will not have, and cannot have, healthy relationships with anyone — including the Church and her leaders and her members — unless we have a relationship with Christ. To the extent that we do not have it, the inherent weakness, the tendency to dissipation in material and mortal things, will prevail.

"When Our Lord puts us through a fiery trial, it is because He knows we need this; we need to *meet Him there.* A priest once said in the confessional: 'The place where you are hurting is the place where Jesus wants to meet you. His wounds are your refuge: they have the power to heal your wounds.' But they will not do so if we are busy fleeing Him, tearing out our hair, and questioning whether He loves us or cares about us. That is how we cut ourselves off from *the only place that reality is,* from the only One who sees it and governs it. The only way to have peace is to be in God's presence, because there is no peace outside of Him. Really: none at all. How could there be?

"Our identity is not in being Catholic or in defending the Church but *in being Christ's* (that is what it means to be a "Christian"). Yes, we belong to His Body, but still our fundamental identity is to be His, to be a son in the Son, a beloved son of the Father. 'This is my beloved Son, in whom I am well pleased.' God says that to each

one of us: You, *you* are my beloved son. There is
no healing for wounded sonship and wounded
fatherhood outside of the Father and the Son."

Dr. Peter Kwasniewski, "In the Midst of
Crisis, Be Driven by Faith, Not by Fear"[100]

"Know that the mystery of suffering in our lives
is the sacred ladder by which we will ascend
to the beauty of the Kingdom of Heaven."

Bishop Donald J. Hying, "Fully
Entering into the Triduum"[101]

"When a devil appeared to her, Catherine
declared her willingness to suffer anything for
Christ. He fled at once.... She died at the age of
thirty-three, having offered all of her sufferings
for the unity of the Church, then in schism."

On St. Catherine of Siena, "Saints
Who Overcame Temptation"[102]

"Almost everything is purified by blood, and without
the shedding of blood there is no forgiveness of sins."

Hebrews 9:22

---

[100] Peter Kwasniewski, "In the Midst of Crisis, Be Driven by Faith, Not by Fear," *Crisis Magazine,* July 19, 2021, https://crisismagazine.com/opinion/in-the-midst-of-crisis-be-driven-by-faith-not-by-fear.

[101] Bishop Donald J. Hying, "Fully Entering into the Triduum," *Simply Catholic,* https://www.simplycatholic.com/how-to-enter-fully-into-the-triduum-this-week/#:~:text=The%20Triduum%20is%20a%20time,Bishop%20Donald%20J..

[102] "Saints Who Overcame Temptation," in Magnificat 23, no. 13 (March 2022), 59.

"For God so loved the world that he gave
his only Son, that whoever believes in him
should not perish but have eternal life."

John 3:16

# Prayers for the Joyful Warrior

## Beneath Thy Protection (*Sub Tuum Praesidium*)

We fly to thy protection, O Holy Mother of God; do not despise our petitions in our necessities, but deliver us always from all dangers, O Glorious and Blessed Virgin. Amen.

## Chaplet of Divine Mercy

*(Using rosary beads, begin by making the sign of the cross)*

You expired, Jesus, but the source of life gushed forth for souls, and the ocean of mercy opened up for the whole world. O Fount of Life, unfathomable Divine Mercy, envelop the whole world and empty Yourself out upon us.

O Blood and Water, which gushed forth from the Heart of Jesus as a fountain of Mercy for us, I trust in You! *(Repeat three times)*

*(Pray one Our Father, one Hail Mary, and the Apostle's Creed)*

*On each large "Our Father" bead, pray:* Eternal Father, I offer You the Body and Blood, soul and divinity of Your dearly beloved Son, our Lord Jesus Christ, in atonement for our sins and those of the whole world.

*On each of the ten, smaller "Hail Mary" beads, pray:* For the sake of His sorrowful Passion, have mercy on us and on the whole world.

*(Repeat for all five decades)*

*Concluding prayer:* Holy God, Holy Mighty One, Holy Immortal One, have mercy on us and on the whole world. *(Say three times)*

Eternal God, in whom mercy is endless and the treasury of compassion inexhaustible, look kindly upon us and increase Your mercy in us, that in difficult moments we might not despair nor become despondent, but with great confidence submit ourselves to Your holy will, which is Love and Mercy itself. Amen.

## CHAPLET OF ST. MICHAEL THE ARCHANGEL[103]

*(Begin by calling on God to be present with you)*

O God, come to my assistance. O Lord, make haste to help me.

Glory be to the Father, and to the Son, and to the Holy Spirit. As it was in the beginning, is now, and ever shall be, world without end.

*(Now make the Nine Salutations in honor of the nine Choirs of Angels. After each salutation, pray one Our Father and three Hail Marys.)*

By the intercession of St. Michael and the celestial Choir of Seraphim, may the Lord make us worthy to burn with the fire of perfect charity. Amen. *(Our Father, three Hail Marys)*

By the intercession of St. Michael and the celestial Choir of Cherubim, may the Lord grant us the grace to leave the ways of sin and run in the paths of Christian perfection. Amen. *(Our Father, three Hail Marys)*

By the intercession of St. Michael and the celestial Choir of Thrones, may the Lord infuse into our hearts a true and sincere spirit of humility. Amen. *(Our Father, three Hail Marys)*

---

[103] Cate Von Dohlen, "How to Pray the St. Michael Chaplet," *Hallow,* https://hallow.com/blog/how-to-pray-the-st-michael-chaplet/ #How-to-pray-St-Michael-Chaplet.

By the intercession of St. Michael and the celestial Choir of Dominations, may the Lord give us grace to govern our senses and overcome any unruly passions. Amen. *(Our Father, three Hail Marys)*

By the intercession of St. Michael and the celestial Choir of Virtues, may the Lord preserve us from evil and falling into temptation. Amen. *(Our Father, three Hail Marys)*

By the intercession of St. Michael and the celestial Choir of Powers, may the Lord protect our souls against the snares and temptations of the devil. Amen. *(Our Father, three Hail Marys)*

By the intercession of St. Michael and the celestial Choir of Principalities, may God fill our souls with a true spirit of obedience. Amen. *(Our Father, three Hail Marys)*

By the intercession of St. Michael and the celestial Choir of Archangels, may the Lord give us perseverance in faith and in all good works in order that we may attain the glory of Heaven. Amen. *(Our Father, three Hail Marys)*

By the intercession of St. Michael and the celestial Choir of Angels, may the Lord grant us to be protected by them in this mortal life and conducted in the life to come to Heaven. Amen. *(Our Father, three Hail Marys)*

*(Say one Our Father in honor of St. Michael the Archangel)*

Our Father, who art in Heaven …

*(Say one Our Father in honor of St. Gabriel the Archangel)*

Our Father, who art in Heaven …

*(Say one Our Father in honor of St. Raphael the Archangel)*

Our Father, who art in Heaven …

*(Say one Our Father in honor of your Guardian Angel)*

Our Father, who art in Heaven ...

*(Conclude your time with God and St. Michael
the Archangel with the following prayers)*

O glorious prince St. Michael, chief and commander of the heavenly hosts, guardian of souls, vanquisher of rebel spirits, servant in the house of the Divine King, and our admirable conductor, you who shine with excellence and superhuman virtue, deliver us from all evil, who turn to you with confidence, and enable us by your gracious protection to serve God more and more faithfully every day. Pray for us, O glorious St. Michael, Prince of the Church of Jesus Christ, that we may be made worthy of His promises.

Almighty and Everlasting God, who, by a prodigy of goodness and a merciful desire for the salvation of all men, has appointed the most glorious Archangel St. Michael Prince of Your Church, make us worthy, we ask You, to be delivered from all our enemies, that none of them may harass us at the hour of death, but that we may be conducted by him into Your Presence. This we ask through the merits of Jesus Christ Our Lord. Amen.

## THE EXORCISM PRAYER OF ST. ANTHONY

Behold, the Cross of the Lord!
Begone, all evil powers!
The Lion of the tribe of Judah,
The Root of David, has conquered!
Alleluia, Alleluia!

## THE EXORCISM PRAYER OF THE ST. BENEDICT MEDAL

May the Holy Cross be my light, may the dragon never be my guide.

Begone, Satan, never tempt me with your vanities; what you offer me
is evil, drink the poison yourself.

## LITANY OF HUMILITY

O Jesus, meek and humble of heart,
Hear me.
From the desire of being esteemed,
Deliver me, O Jesus.
From the desire of being loved,
Deliver me, O Jesus.
From the desire of being extolled,
Deliver me, O Jesus.
From the desire of being honored,
Deliver me, O Jesus.
From the desire of being praised,
Deliver me, O Jesus.
From the desire of being preferred to others,
Deliver me, O Jesus.
From the desire of being consulted,
Deliver me, O Jesus.
From the desire of being approved,
Deliver me, O Jesus.
From the fear of being humiliated,
Deliver me, O Jesus.
From the fear of being despised,
Deliver me, O Jesus.
From the fear of suffering rebukes,
Deliver me, O Jesus.
From the fear of being calumniated,
Deliver me, O Jesus.
From the fear of being forgotten,

Deliver me, O Jesus.
From the fear of being ridiculed,
Deliver me, O Jesus.
From the fear of being wronged,
Deliver me, O Jesus.
From the fear of being suspected,
Deliver me, O Jesus.
That others may be loved more than I,
Jesus, grant me the grace to desire it.
That others may be esteemed more than I,
Jesus, grant me the grace to desire it.
That, in the opinion of the world, others may increase and I may
decrease,
Jesus, grant me the grace to desire it.
That others may be chosen and I set aside,
Jesus, grant me the grace to desire it.
That others may be praised and I go unnoticed,
Jesus, grant me the grace to desire it.
That others may be preferred to me in everything,
Jesus, grant me the grace to desire it.
That others may become holier than I, provided that I may become
as holy as I should,
Jesus, grant me the grace to desire it.

## The Memorare

Remember, O most gracious Virgin Mary, that never was it known that anyone who fled to thy protection, implored thy help, or sought thy intercession, was left unaided. Inspired by this confidence I fly unto thee, O Virgin of virgins, my Mother. To thee do I come, before thee I kneel, sinful and sorrowful. O Mother of the Word Incarnate, despise not my petitions, but in thy mercy hear and answer me. Amen.

## Morning Offering

O Jesus, through the Immaculate Heart of Mary, I offer you my prayers, works, joys, and sufferings of this day for all the intentions of your Sacred Heart in union with the Holy Sacrifice of the Mass throughout the world, for the salvation of souls, the reparation of sins, the reunion of all Christians, and in particular for the intentions of the Holy Father this month. Amen.

## Prayer for Deliverance from Evil[104]

Immaculate Heart! Help us to conquer the menace of evil, which so easily takes root in the hearts of the people of today, and whose immeasurable effects already weigh down upon our modern world and seem to block the paths towards the future!

From famine and war, deliver us.

From nuclear war, from incalculable self-destruction, from every kind of war, deliver us.

From sins against the life of man from its very beginning, deliver us.

From hatred and from the demeaning of the dignity of the children of God, deliver us.

From every kind of injustice in the life of society, both national and international, deliver us.

From readiness to trample on the commandments of God, deliver us.

From attempts to stifle in human hearts the very truth of God, deliver us.

From the loss of awareness of good and evil, deliver us.

From sins against the Holy Spirit, deliver us, deliver us.

Accept, O Mother of Christ, this cry laden with the sufferings of all individual human beings, laden with the sufferings of whole

---

[104] Pope St. John Paul II, *Consecration of All Individuals and Peoples of the World to the Immaculate Heart of Mary*, 1984.

societies. Help us with the power of the Holy Spirit to conquer all sin: individual sin and the "sin of the world," sin in all its manifestations. Let there be revealed, once more, in the history of the world the infinite saving power of the Redemption: the power of merciful Love! May it put a stop to evil! May it transform consciences! May your Immaculate Heart reveal for all the light of Hope!

## Prayer to Our Lady, Queen of Angels

August Queen of Heaven, sovereign Mistress of the Angels, who didst receive from the beginning the mission and the power to crush the serpent's head, we beseech thee to send thy holy angels, that under thy command and by thy power, they may pursue the evil spirits, encounter them on every side, resist their bold attacks, and drive them hence into the abyss of woe. Most holy Mother, send thy angels to defend us and to drive the cruel enemy from us. All ye holy angels and archangels, help and defend us. Amen. O good and tender Mother! Thou shalt ever be our Love and our Hope. Holy Angels and Archangels, keep and defend us. Amen.

## Prayer to St. Joseph, Terror of Demons

St. Joseph, Terror of Demons, cast your solemn gaze upon the devil and all his minions, and protect us with your mighty staff. You fled through the night to avoid the devil's wicked designs; now with the power of God, smite the demons as they flee from you! Grant special protection, we pray, for children, fathers, families, and the dying. By God's grace, no demon dares approach while you are near, so we beg of you, always be near to us. Amen.

## Prayer to St. Michael the Archangel

St. Michael the Archangel, defend us in battle, be our protection against the wickedness and snares of the devil. May God rebuke him, we humbly pray; and do thou, O Prince of the Heavenly host, by the power of God, cast into hell Satan and all the evil spirits who prowl about the world seeking the ruin of souls. Amen.

## Psalm 91

He who dwells in the shelter of the Most High,
>who abides in the shadow of the Almighty,
will say to the Lord, "My refuge and my fortress;
>my God, in whom I trust."
For he will deliver you from the snare of the fowler
>and from the deadly pestilence;
he will cover you with his pinions,
>and under his wings you will find refuge;
>his faithfulness is a shield and buckler.
You will not fear the terror of the night,
>nor the arrow that flies by day,
nor the pestilence that stalks in darkness,
>nor the destruction that wastes at noonday.
A thousand may fall at your side,
>ten thousand at your right hand;
>but it will not come near you.
You will only look with your eyes
>and see the recompense of the wicked.
Because you have made the Lord your refuge,
>the Most High your habitation,
no evil shall befall you,
>no scourge come near your tent.
For he will give his angels charge of you
>to guard you in all your ways.
On their hands they will bear you up,
>lest you dash your foot against a stone.

You will tread on the lion and the adder,
    the young lion and the serpent you will trample under foot.
Because he cleaves to me in love, I will deliver him;
    I will protect him, because he knows my name.
When he calls to me, I will answer him;
    I will be with him in trouble,
    I will rescue him and honor him.
With long life I will satisfy him,
    and show him my salvation.

# About the Author

Jesse Romero is a full time bilingual Catholic lay evangelist who is nationally recognized for his dynamic Christ-centered preaching. He is a retired Los Angeles deputy sheriff, three-time world police boxing champion and a two-time USA kickboxing champion. Jesse makes the sometimes complex teachings of the Faith understandable with his straight-talk approach. He has a degree from Mount St. Mary's College in Los Angeles and an M.A. in Catholic theology from Franciscan University in Ohio. Recipient of the Archbishop Fulton Sheen Award in 2010 and the Defender of the Faith Award in 2014, Jesse was inducted into the Catholic Sports Hall of Fame in 2015. He hosts two radio podcasts daily on Virgin Most Powerful Radio.

# Sophia Institute

Sophia Institute is a nonprofit institution that seeks to nurture the spiritual, moral, and cultural life of souls and to spread the gospel of Christ in conformity with the authentic teachings of the Roman Catholic Church.

Sophia Institute Press fulfills this mission by offering translations, reprints, and new publications that afford readers a rich source of the enduring wisdom of mankind.

Sophia Institute also operates the popular online resource CatholicExchange.com. *Catholic Exchange* provides world news from a Catholic perspective as well as daily devotionals and articles that will help readers to grow in holiness and live a life consistent with the teachings of the Church.

In 2013, Sophia Institute launched Sophia Institute for Teachers to renew and rebuild Catholic culture through service to Catholic education. With the goal of nurturing the spiritual, moral, and cultural life of souls, and an abiding respect for the role and work of teachers, we strive to provide materials and programs that are at once enlightening to the mind and ennobling to the heart; faithful and complete, as well as useful and practical.

Sophia Institute gratefully recognizes the Solidarity Association for preserving and encouraging the growth of our apostolate over the course of many years. Without their generous and timely support, this book would not be in your hands.

www.SophiaInstitute.com
www.CatholicExchange.com
www.SophiaTeachers.org